10th (S) Battalion

THE SHERWOOD FORESTERS

THE HISTORY OF THE BATTALION DURING THE GREAT WAR

by
Lieut. W. N. Hoyte

EDITED BY
M. T. F. J. McNeela

Published by
The Naval & Military Press Ltd

CONTENTS

List of Officers who proceeded
to France with the Battalion in
July 1915 iv

List of Officers who received
decorations while serving
with the Battalion v

Preface xi

Editor's preface xiii

Chapter I
England 1

Chapter II
France – July 1915 down to the
training for the Somme Battle 5

Chapter III
To the Battle of Arras 13

Chapter IV
Arras and Ypres 1917 28

Chapter V
Cambrai and the March Push 43

Chapter VI
The Return Push 60

Chapter VII
After the Armistice 75

List of Officers
who proceeded to France
with the Battalion in July 1915

Headquarters:-

Lieut. Col. W. E. Banbury
Major J. C. Keown
Capt. & Adjt. G. J. Partridge
Lieut. & Qr. Mr. S. J. Pearsall
Lieut. L. W. Roe. (Signalling Officer)
2/Lt. G. Chapman. (Machine Gun Officer)
2/Lt. R. A. Ruttle. (Transport Officer)
Capt. L. D. Saunders. R.A.M.C.

A. Coy.

Capt. G. P. Goodall
Capt. N. H. Pratt
Lieut. P. E. Cuckow
Lieut. P. Knox-Shaw
2/Lt. J. N. Knight

B. Coy.

Major A. W. Young
Capt. R. H. Gregory
Lieut. J. A. Meads
Lieut. T. M. Willcox
2/Lt. W. N. Hoyte

C. Coy.

Major G. W. Moran
Capt. M. Grimes
Lieut. E. T. R. Carlyon
Lieut. A. G. Shaw
2/Lt. R. C. Wilmot
2/Lt. J. Hutcheson

D. Coy.

Capt. J. W. Fisher
Capt. E. R. Oakden
Lieut. D. W. Ramsay
2/Lt. T. W. Daniel
2/Lt. M. F. M. Wright
2/Lt. E. S. Chandler

List of Officers
who received decorations
while serving with the Battalion

Lieut.-Col. W. E. Banbury C.M.G.
Lieut.- Col. H. J. King D.S.O.
Lieut.-Col. T. W. Daniel D.S.O. and bar M.C.
Major C. H. Page D.S.O.
Capt. & Qr. Mr. S. J. Pearsall O.B.E.
Capt. W. J. Fisher D.S.O.
Capt. J. A. Meads M.C.
Capt. J. N. Knight M.C.
Capt. L. Jacques M.C. and bar
Capt. W. E. Brandt M.C.
Capt. G. C. Winckley M.C. and bar
Capt. A. J. M. Lander M.C.
Capt. F. B. Joyce M.C.
Capt. R. A. Barker M.C.
Capt. J. Ross M.C.
Capt. L. D. Saunders (R.A.M.C.) M.C.
Capt. Rev. V. T. S. Jagg (C.F.) M.C.
Lieut. W. N. Hoyte M.C. and bar
Lieut. H. E. Hodding M.C.
Lieut. S. C. Day M.C.
Lieut. C. F. S. Cox M.C.
2nd Lt. G. B. Greenwood D.S.O.
2nd Lt. R. S. Whyatt M.C.
2nd Lt. W. C. Wicks M.C.
2nd Lt. C. K. Hanson M.C.
2nd Lt. J. W. Bowmer M.C.

During the time spent in France, many decorations were awarded to N.C.O's and men of the battalion. Unfortunately it has been found impossible to secure a complete copy of the Battalion Daily Orders, and many names may unfortunately be missing from the following list. In addition to this list a few names have been mentioned in the history itself, but to those gallant fellows whose names are omitted our humblest apologies are tendered:

The following officers were mentioned in Despatches at various times:

Lieut.-Col. W. E. Banbury C.M.G., D.S.O.
Lieut.-Col. H. J. King D.S.O.
Lieut.-Col. T. W. Daniel D.S.O., M.C.
Major C. H. Page D.S.O.
Capt. J. W. Fisher D.S.O.
Capt. & Qr. Mr. S. J. Pearsall O.B.E.
Capt. J. A. Meads M.C.
Capt. T. P. C. Wilson

Awarded the D.C.M. for gallantry on September 25th, 1915:

Lce. Cpl. E. Mosley
Pte. E. Jordan

Awarded the D.C.M. for gallantry on February 15th, 1916:

Sergt. F. Wright
Lce. Cpl. R. Cox
Sergt. J. Sandy
Pte. A. Denton
Sergt. A. A. Morris

Awarded the D.C.M. for gallantry on March 2nd, 1916:

Cpl. B. Brewer
Pte. H. Bradshaw
Pte. W. Dove

Awarded the D.C.M. in the Gazette dated 3/6/16:

Cpl. A. Salt

Awarded the Military Medal in the Gazette dated 11/10/16:

Sergt. A. B. Caunt
Cpl. G. Tongue
Cpl. H. Meer
Cpl. W. J. Morriss
Lce. Cpl. E. H. Harlow
Pte. E. J. Adams
Pte. S. J. Canwell
Pte. A. L. Green

Awarded the Military Medal in the Gazette dated 21/10/16:

Pte. A. Tucker
Pte. J. H. Rushton
Pte. E. Odam
Pte. W. Wright
Pte. J. W. Robinson
Pte. J. Robinson
Pte. T. Sheldon
Pte. C. Wood
Pte. H. Dalby

Awarded the D.C.M. in the Gazette dated 16/1/17:

Lce. Cpl. E. Hawley

Awarded the Military Medal for gallantry on April 23rd, 1917:

Sergt. G. V. Kerry
Pte. J. Hill
Lce. Cpl. A. Adams

Awarded the following decorations for gallantry on August 5th, 1917:

Sergt. H. Dalby M.M. Bar to M.M.
Cpl. W. Alton M.M.

Awarded the Military Medal for gallantry on September 16th, 1917:

Sergt. W. Guy
Pte. J. H. Paling
Pte. J. Harding
Pte. F. White

Awarded the D.C.M. in the Gazette dated 19/11/17:

Sergt. C. Coomber
Sergt. T. Dove

Awarded the Military Medal in the Gazette dated 14/1/18:

Cpl. G. Woodhouse
Pte. W. Newton
Pte. H. E. Lane
Pte. W. Johnson
Pte. P. S. Holmes
Pte. H. Ginger
Pte. S. Lamb

Awarded the Military Medal in the Gazette dated 13/5/18:

Sergt. S. Scaife
Sergt. H. Huckerby
Lce. Cpl. S. Flint
Pte. J. Sawyer
Pte. S. Lamb M.M., Bar to M.M.

Awarded the D.C.M. in the Gazette dated 22/11/18:

Coy. Sergt. Major S. Scaife M.M.
Pte. S. C. Smith.

Awarded the Military Medal in the Gazette dated 18/11/18:

Sergt. E. J. Bawcutt
Cpl. F. J. Chadderton
Cpl. W. Dean
Pte. W. Clegg

Pte. A. Gascoyne
Pte. A. Mawyer
Pte. W. Godber
Pte. W. H. Sutton

Awarded the D.C.M. in the Gazette dated 31/12/18:

Sergt. W. Young
Lce. Cpl. V. Rose
Pte. F. Hindes

Awarded the Silver Medal for Bravery by H.M. The King of Montenegro - Gazette 9/3/17:

Pte. J. Betts

Awarded the Croix de Guerre in the Gazette dated 25/2/18:

Sergt. F. Malthouse

The undermentioned are a few of those who were 'Mentioned in Despatches':

R.Q.M.S. V. J. C. Hickman
Cpl. C. G. Wyld
Lce. Cpl. E. H. Johnson
Pte. C. Hollingsworth
Pte. E. Morgan
Sergt. G. White
Sergt. A..B. Caunt
Pte. P. H. Whittaker
Sergt. J. W. Furniss
Pte. E. Scotham

Preface

At last, after many weeks of toil, the History of the 10th Sherwood Foresters has been written. Perhaps the history may appear to some readers to be uninteresting or even lacking in detail, but it has been very difficult to obtain all the information which is necessary to make a battle sound realistic on paper, and again - time has been short.

I am confident, however, that all officers and men who served in the battalion and who peruse this history will agree with me that it is a work of art, and that the literary effort and fine touches of humour from the author's pen are worthy of the highest praise. The history was written by Lieut. N. W. Hoyte, M.C., while spending a well-earned summer holiday on the north coast of Scotland before resuming his studies at Cambridge University, and the other two officers who served throughout the whole war with the Battalion – Capt. S. J. Pearsall, O.B.E. and myself – were only too glad to be of some assistance to him in reading through the proofs. I feel sure that everyone connected with the Battalion will congratulate Lieut. Hoyte most heartily on his work which will be cherished by all as a most valuable souvenir of the Great War.

T. W. Daniel

Editor's Preface

In the immediate post war years, with the aftermath of the horror and tragedy of the Great War still fresh in the mind, many unit histories were written, for the most part by those who participated and survived. Some had much to admire in their literary style and attention to detail, others were written by egotists who seemed to have forgotten the original reason for the work, to perpetuate the memory of the unit. One thing they had in common is that they were published.

For some unknown reason this history failed to see the light of day and has remained unpublished for 80 years. However, I feel that any true account of the doings of a unit whatever its merits or otherwise, deserves its rightful place in the literature of the Great War. The words penned by a surviving soldier will ultimately come from a soul which has experienced the horrors of Hell. Works written in recent times, no matter how academic, are vicarious.

It is with this in mind that I have wished to present this history of the 10th Battalion The Sherwood Foresters in its unedited form.

M. T. F. J. McNeela
4th August 2002

CHAPTER I
England

The beginnings and the early days of the New Armies in 1914 will soon become legendary; one can imagine historians in days to come shaking their heads doubtfully over the facts, wondering if there has not been an '0' too many in that figure, or if this fact has not been a trifle exaggerated. But the historians at the present time are handicapped for there was no Battalion War Diary when in England and private diarists were few.

The 10th Sherwood Foresters first concentrated as a Battalion at Wool in Dorset, a rough crowd of men in 'civvies' all eager to get their khaki, lay hands on a rifle and get across to France with as little delay as possible.

Captain Stackhouse, a regular officer of the Sherwood Foresters, arrived to take command of the Battalion. This officer was a martinet of the very best type and a leader of men. No rations of any description were forthcoming on the first day. Captain Stackhouse ordered the men to go into the woods and villages and forage for themselves. And so they did; and greater wonder still - they all returned to camp that night not at all disheartened. It seemed to them an amusing way to spend a day, but tomorrow they might get on with the real training.

Captain (then Lieut.) S. J. Pearsall - the inimitable 'Willie' - arrived as Quartermaster to the Battalion in the first of those early days; (rations were always forthcoming after Willie's arrival). Roe and Pratt (then 2nd Lieuts.) were also among the early arrivals. Later Major J. C. Keown arrived as second in command of the Battalion, wearing a bowler hat and carrying an umbrella! This little group of officers had, for a short time, the enormously responsible task of licking the men into shape to resemble a battalion, of dividing up the battalion into companies and platoons, and all the other thousand and one things which have to be done when a battalion is home. The huge task was done and well done, even in 1916 some of the old hands would talk of the iron discipline which Captain Stackhouse required. However, Captain Stackhouse eventually rejoined the 1st Battalion (he was afterwards killed at Neuve Chapelle), and Lieut.-Col. W. E. Banbury of the Indian Army arrived to command the Battalion.

The 10th Sherwood Foresters formed one of the battalions of the 51st Infantry Brigade, 17th Division. The Divisional Commander was Major-General T. D. Pilcher, C.B. Brigadier-General Kay commanded the 51st Brigade until June 1915, but was then replaced by Brigadier-General Fell. Other battalions in the Brigade were:-

7th Lincolnshire Regt.
7th Border Regt.
and 8th South Staffordshire Regt.

Other officers joined in large numbers. Captain G. J. Partridge was appointed Adjutant, and the companies were commanded Captain Goodall (A), Major Young (B), Major Moran (C), and Captain Walker (D).

Towards the end of the year, the N.C.O's and men of 'C' Company were removed 'en bloc' to the 12th Pioneer Battalion Sherwood Foresters, and they were replaced by a company of men who had been recruited in Nottingham, the result of an unsuccessful attempt to raise a battalion there. These men were mostly clerks, and of a distinctly superior education to the men of the other companies who were chiefly Derbyshire miners. The difference was very apparent, especially as the new men arrived with khaki greatcoats, while the original men were still in blue uniforms.

The camp which had been in August 1914 established at Bovington - 3 miles from Wool Station - was moved in October to Lulworth - about 7 miles due south, on the Dorset coast. The weather was wretched in the new camp, and there was only very inadequate canvas for both officers and men. A certain regiment of the same Brigade organised a strike - presumably against the weather when conditions were at their worst, but this movement met with no encouragement from the Sherwood Foresters.

A further move was made to another site near Lulworth, and again early in December we moved back to Bovington. It was found impossible to escape from the mud, but an efficient system of drains was dug (Lieut. Giles being O.C. Drains), so that conditions actually in the camp were tolerable. The drains formed a series of crevasses zig-zagging in all directions, and it was an incentive to sobriety in the Mess to know that half a dozen slippery rickety duckboards, bridging black chasms, had to be crossed before one's tent was reached.

Huts were slowly erected for the men at Bovington early in the New year, the officers, however, remained under canvas in a little pine wood close by. Ranges had been dug by the R.E., and in February a sufficient number of short rifles had arrived to make musketry possible. Early in April the battalion moved to a canvas camp close to Lulworth; the weather rapidly improved and the whole of the Spring was spent here. It was a wonderful time of the year; close to the camp were woods carpeted with primroses, and the bluebells later filled the hollow with a blue haze.

On the hot afternoons the whole battalion bathed on the beach at Durdle Door.

Brigade and Divisional training took place, and the memory of those long, jolly, healthy days remains sweet even now. One scheme closely resembled war conditions when the Battalion marched some 10 miles one evening and relieved a battalion of the 50th Brigade in a system of trenches close to Wareham. The whole of the next day was spent in these trenches, playing at trench-warfare; reliefs took place in the evening and after the long march we arrived in camp soon after dawn on the next day.

By this time officers' charges - strong little cobs - and mules had arrived; the weird braying of these American mules at night kept one awake for some time.

From the very early days rumours were constantly arising about the date of our crossing to France. It was the inexhaustible topic of conversation, and the date always seemed to keep cleverly about two months ahead. After a series of very authentic rumours about a move to Sutton Veny, the Division was moved at the end of May to the outskirts of Winchester. The battalions all went by march route, bivouacking each night. The 10th Sherwood Foresters marched for five consecutive days in splendid weather and through lovely country; nights were spent at Bovington, Cranborough Park, a little wood near Ringwood, and finally in the fields round Totton near Southampton. On May 30th Flowerdown Camp close to Winchester was reached. This was occupied by the Battalion until they left for France. Very little training on a large scale was done here owing to the close nature of the country, but a system of trenches was dug close to the camp and inter - battalion reliefs were practised again and again in these. The short Lee - Enfield rifles for the men arrived here; before that time about ninety per cent of the rifles had been D.P. (Drill Purpose). A large amount of musketry was fired on ranges several miles away, and Major-General Pilcher superintended a few days field firing. All the final equipment for the Battalion came in with a rush, Lewis guns, signalling equipment, and the rest.

Finally about July 10th the magic order arrived to prepare to move overseas. This of course caused huge excitement. Some lucky men were granted forty eight hours leave. The next morning the entire Battalion appeared at the Orderly Room and demanded a similar amount of leave. Fortunately it was possible to grant this, and officers and men went off in two batches for a very hurried farewell to those at home. There were no absentees on July 14th when the companies paraded for entrainment. The transport went via Southampton and Havre; the companies travelled to Folkestone, and on the night of July 14/15th crossed to Boulogne.

CHAPTER II

France - July 1915
Down to the training for the Somme battle

The 10th Sherwood Foresters landed at Boulogne early in the morning of July 15th On disembarkation they marched to St. Martin's Camp on a hill about the town. Iron rations were given to all officers and men while here, and we sent home our first Field Service postcards; delightful things which form the lazy man's letter. In the afternoon, the Battalion Marched to Pont de Briques Station; we were all very green, and most of the men insisted on marching on the left of the road from force of habit.

The Battalion entrained at the station for St. Omer which was reached about midnight July 15/16th Here the transport rejoined us; they had started for overseas one day before the Battalion. We were a very tired lot of men who marched to Zudausques where we billeted. On the march in the early dawn we heard the first gun miles away eastwards.

From this village the Battalion marched in two days, starting on the 18th to Caestre, a village some ten kilometres north-east of Hazebrook.

The sun was infernally hot, and this - combined with the unspeakable pavé roads - made marching a torture for most men. There was a feeling of being very much closer to the war at Caestre, the mutter of the guns could be heard all the time, and on clear evenings the 'Archie' bursts could be seen round Hun planes over the line.

A lazy week was spent here; it included an inspection by General Plumer, commanding the Second Army. 'Willie' Pearsall's feats of equitation on 'Grandma' at this parade cannot go unmentioned!

We learnt that we were destined to go to the famous Salient for the first experiences of trench warfare and so no one expected it to be a 'joyride' in any sense.

On the night July 25/26th the battalion marched via Mont des cats to a camp immediately south of Reninghelst, close to the windmill on the Locre road. Coming over the Mont we could see the very lights rising all along the line, and a super-cautious officer ordered 'no smoking', 'no singing'!

'A' Company, commanded by Captain G. P. Goodall, went on the 27th for a tour of instruction to the 7th Battalion Sherwood Foresters, who were holding trenches in Sanctuary Wood. The tour was planned to last for 48 hours, but the enemy began active operations on the immediate left of the sector with liquid fire on the night 28/29th, and the company accordingly remained in the line for five days. Meanwhile, 'B' and 'C' companies each went for 24 hours instruction to trenches held by the 52nd Brigade near St. Eloi. Neither instructors nor instructed knew much about trench warfare, but the line was fortunately quiet at that time.

Further operations by the enemy astride the Ypres - Menin Road caused the 17th Division to move up into a position of readiness to meet any further attacks.

On August 1st the battalion moved to Belgian chateau near Kruistraat, and routes were reconnoitred in readiness to move in support of the Sanctuary Wood sector.

The activity in this part of the line, however, ceased, and a move was made to huts at Ouderdom and thence again to Reninghelst. From here the battalion relieved the 7th East Yorkshire Regiment (50th Brigade) in trenches immediately south of the Ypres - Comines canal on the night August 15/16th, and this sector was occupied until the night 27/28th Captain Gregory and Captain Oakden were both slightly wounded, while 2nd Lieut. Wilmot was badly hit by a shell; he rejoined the battalion about a year later. On the whole it was a very quiet trip.

With only two days rest the 10th Sherwood Foresters and the 7th Border Regt. were lent to the 9th Brigade (3rd Division), and on the evening August 31st they marched past General Plumer and on up to Sanctuary Wood, relieving troops of the 9th Brigade in trenches A4 to A11. This sector was held till September 14th It was a 'hot' place, Sanctuary Wood was never a quiet spot and casualties were constantly occurring. The most bitter of these were major A. W. Young and 2nd Lieut. J. Hutcheson - both killed. They were both such types, the one of the old school turning out for this war to find in it his youth, and the other the boy getting his commission, and in doing so becoming a grown man. In the one we seemed to lose a father, in the other a brother.

From September 15th to 20th the battalion had a well-earned rest in the Reninghelst Camp.

On the night September 21/22nd they again relieved troops of the 9th Brigade in the same part of Sanctuary Wood. 2nd Lieut. R. O. Nevitt and 2nd Lieut. T. A. Nichols joined the battalion and the 24th A minor operation was carried out on the 25th on the immediate left to synchronise with the main attack at Loos. The wood was heavily shelled and the Regimental Aid Post had a narrow escape, but casualties were comparatively light. In the afternoon of the 29th a large mine was exploded by the enemy on our immediate left followed by a small attack. The same evening the battalion was relieved by troops of the 3rd Division and withdrew to the Reninghelst Camp. The bombers remained behind to take part in the counter-attack on the mine crater. Lieut. J. A. Meads won the Military Cross for gallantry in this fight.

During these two tours Lieut. T. M. Willcox had a series of miraculous escapes in Sanctuary Wood; the Hun seemed to have worked up a special and particular hate against this unfortunate officer, but he defied all attempts to suppress him. Twice or three times 5.9 shells burst close alongside him, and on September 26th a sniper's bullet just grazed the skin off his nose and cheek.

From October 2nd To the 4th 'B' and 'C' companies were used as reserve troops to the 51st Brigade in the vicinity of Verbrandenmolen. They were relieved by troops of the 9th Division, and on October 6th the whole battalion moved to billets in Eecke and Caestre expecting to move down to the Loos area; this move, however, never took place.

On October 21st the battalion moved back again to the Salient, to hold the 'B' trenches in Sanctuary Wood. The line was quieter than before, and the main enemy was the weather. A sniper proved annoying at the beginning of this tour, and Captain J. W. Fisher started his series of wounds with a bullet from this Hun, but Lieut. T. W. Daniel stopped his sniping for ever with a clever shot early one morning. But trenches gradually fell in, in spite of all our labours. All ranks came to know the unspeakable Flanders mud; it was scooped patiently over the parados, but one might as well have tried to bale the ocean with a teacup - so bottomless was it.

Lieut. J. N. Knight was severely wounded in Poperinghe on October 4th by a high velocity shell; he rejoined the battalion about a year later.

The Battalion was in huts from October 30th to November 9th near Ouderdom, it then moved up to the Ypres ramparts and vicinity as the reserve battalion to the 51st Brigade, who held a portion of the line from Hooge northwards to Railway Wood. The Brigade continued to hold this front until January 6th and the battalion worked periodical reliefs with the 7th Lincolnshire Regiment. There were occasional blessed visits to the camp at Ouderdom for a wash and a change of clothes at the baths on the Vlamertinghe road. Destructive shoots on the enemy front line became positively monotonous, and the mud got deeper and deeper. We all paddled about cheerily in 'gumboots thigh' and woolly jackets, and cursed the Hun and all his activities. The sound of 18 inch shells about to drop near the Cloth Hall caused many of us to sprint a hundred yards into the shelter of the ramparts in almost level time.

The most outstanding event for the month was the gas attack by the enemy on December 19th The battalion was then in the Ouderdom Camp and was alarmed in the very early morning by the gunfire; the troops moved up to a position of readiness by the Ypres ramparts through the town which was full of tear gas and was being heavily shelled. The situation was, however, quiet on our front and after a hungry noisy day we marched back to the Ouderdom Camp. It seems impossible to convey in a few words the atmosphere and the temper of the battalion while in these trenches; there was everything to make for depression; Lieut. A. G. Shaw was killed, the weather was unspeakable, the fatigues for the R. E. and tunnellers seemed endless and heart-breaking; and yet given a night in camp or in cellars, a packet of letters from home or a rum ration, and the men were ready to meet the Devil himself.

Troops of the 24th Division relieved the 10th Sherwood Foresters on January 6th, and the latter went by train and march route to Houlle and Moulle (villages west of St. Omer). Here they stayed till February 8th resting and training. The 17th Division relieved the 3rd Division in the 'Bluff' and Hill 60 sector of the line on the 8th, and the battalion moved on that date to a position of reserve, a camp north of La Clytte.

On the night February 13/14th they relieved the 7th Lincolnshire Regiment who were holding the Bluff and trenches immediately north of the Ypres - Comines canal. The spoil from this canal when it was dug was heaped upon either side, and thin pine woods were grown on the mounds; a great accumulation of spoil, rising considerably above the level of the rest of the ridge was known as the Bluff. To the south east of the side facing the enemy it presented a very stiff face, to the north west it sloped away more gradually in the long heap known as Spoil Bank. The face towards the enemy was full of snipers' posts, and men from here were able to completely overlook the German front trenches which ran almost at the foot of the Bluff.

From the top of the Bluff a very extensive view behind our lines was obtained; on a clear day Abeele Aerodrome could be seen, about a dozen miles away. A low ridge of ground stretched away in a north-easterly direction from the Bluff; our front trenches were about 100 yards over the crest of the ridge; on its crest and westerly side were our support lines and Reserve Wood - a tangled mass of undergrowth and tree stumps about 200 yards from east to west. The possession of the crest of this ridge would give the enemy good observation, but not so good as from the top of the Bluff.

Major J. C. Keown was in command of the battalion as Lieut.-Col. Banbury was on leave at the time. All ranks were wearing steel helmets for the first time. The next 24 hours tested the fighting qualities of the battalion severely. The relief was a quiet one. About 8.30 am. on the next morning a slow bombardment of our front and support lines started, and the enemy apparently registered these lines with all his available artillery, trench mortars and rifle grenades. At about 2.30 p.m. the bomdardment suddenly assumed tremendous intensity, every bit of Hun frightfulness seemed to be going off at once. This continued for about two hours; all telephonic communication with the front line was soon cut, but the seriousness of the shelling could be seen from Bn. H.Q. which was in Spoil Bank, about 600 yards west of the Bluff. Artillery retaliation was called for but this proved to be quite inadequate. The Divisional artillery had only just completed their relief the night before and their guns were not accurately registered; the sound-deafening effect of a strong west wind was also very marked, and unless one was actually in sight of the bombardment, or worse still in the middle of it, it was very difficult to realise that anything serious was occurring.

At about 5.40 p.m. a mine was exploded under the trenches occupied by 'C' Company which unfortunately caused many casualties to our men. This was followed by an enemy attack which reached our front line but was unable to make any further headway. Some of the enemy reached the top of the Bluff. Several immediate counter attacks [were made] by our bombers under Lieut. Daniel, assisted by the bombers of the Lincolnshire Regt. under Lieut. Jones, but without success, Lieut. Daniel being wounded. The 7th Border Regt. and two companies of the 7th Lincolnshire Regt. reinforced our line with a view to counter-attack at 7pm. but no impression could be made on the enemy who had evidently established himself firmly. The arrival of trench mortar ammunition had unfortunately been allowed to dwindle to ridiculously small dimensions by the relieved division.

Captain J. W. Fisher did magnificent work on the left flank of the battalion in command of 'D' Company. He was awarded the D.S.O. for his gallantry which undoubtedly prevented the enemy from gaining a footing in Reserve Wood.

The battalion was withdrawn to a support position on February 15th and was relieved, very tired and battered, on the night of 16/17th by troops of the 3rd Division. They marched to a camp north of La Clytte where the extent of the casualties was ascertained for the first time. These had been very heavy, 16 officers and 334 other ranks. It was melancholy work piecing together the story of the fight and finding out what had happened to the missing.

All the officers of 'B' Company were either killed or missing. Lieut. D. W. Ramsay was known to have been killed, also Captain G. P. Goodall; they were both officers who had been with the battalion from its very early days. The last that was seen of Lieut. P. Knox-Shaw (who proved to be wounded and prisoner) was at the head of a bombing counter attack up one of the communication trenches. Captain E. T. R. Carlyon was wounded a little while before the attack and was left in a shelter; he was also taken prisoner. Of the others, 2nd Lieuts. Chandler - Ebery - & Melville - little definite news could be obtained, presumably they were killed.

During the whole operations, the M.O. - Captain L. D. Saunders worked wonders at the R.A.P.; he was awarded the Military Cross for his untiring devotion to duty. Lieut. T. W. Daniel was also awarded the Military Cross. In this attack the enemy had secured observation of our back areas, but he undoubtedly expected to gain more ground.

While in the camp at La Clytte the battalion was reinforced and reorganised. Lieuts. T. P. C. Wilson and W. H. Nelson joined here amongst others. This camp was occupied until the deliberate counter-attack on the lost positions was made by the 3rd Division on March 2nd. On February 29th the battalion moved to dugouts in Spoil Bank and performed mighty feats of weight lifting in carrying up huge trench mortar bombs to the front line. At 4.20 am. on the 2nd. The attack was launched and was a complete success, some of the original German front line being captured in addition to our own lost portion. In the afternoon the battalion bombers reinforced the 8th King's Own who were holding the 'German Bean' which had been captured that morning; they remained there until relieved some thirty hours later. The battalion was relieved on the night 3/4th and withdrew again to the camp North of la Clytte, thence on March 6th they marched to La Creche (East of Bailleul), the 17th Division being transferred to the 2nd Corps. Thus after about seven months' trench warfare in the Salient we turned our backs on it for more than a year. Our only regret was that we had not killed more Huns. We were all by now well hardened to the sights and sounds of the modern battle, and the time from now till July was spent comparatively uneventfully, preparing for the long agony of the Somme.

The stay at La Creche lasted until March 19th when the battalion marched to Armentieres and occupied billets there until the 27th They then relieved the 7th Lincolnshire Regt. in the sector of the line immediately North of the Armentieres - Lille Road. This part of the line was held alternately with the Lincolnshire Regt. until May 13th It was on the whole a pleasant life; in the trenches the men could see the results of their work and there was never an undue amount of 'frightfulness'. There were 'unhealthy' spots; for instance that terrifying corner where the wire always required mending and across which a German machine gun would open fire at any moment, but compared with the Salient it was a rest cure.

And in Armentieres - those were the palmy days when the shelling of the town was an event to make everyone feel very indignant and surprised. There were beds with sheets, the teashop, Café Saute Barbe, and the 'pictures'.

While in these trenches Capt. L. Gilbert joined the battalion, and took up command of 'D' company. Lieut. W. N. Hoyte took up the duties of bombing officer on the 51st Brigade Headquarters.

Lieut. S. C. Day had a wonderful escape one afternoon; while looking over the front line parapet he was fired at by a German sniper; the bullet penetrated the top of the dome of his steel helmet, was deflected downwards inside the helmet, and wounded him in the small of the back.

On May 13th the 17th Division was relieved by the New Zealand Division, and for the next four days the battalion moved by road to a training area West of St. Omer; billets were occupied at Houlle. The period from May 18th to June 11th was devoted to intensive training; this meant hard work for all ranks - a very early breakfast, then out with the cookers to the training area near Inglinghem Mill. The weather was good for the most part, and the men grew hard and fit. The battalion moved down to the Somme area by train on June 12th as well trained as they really could be. 2nd Lieut. F. B. Joyce joined the battalion during this training period.

A canvas camp at Allonville (North of Amiens) was occupied after detrainment at Longpre. Lieut. T. P. C. Wilson did such wonders with the advance party in 'winning' tents that the staff evidently thought that he might be dangerous with a battalion, and removed him to the sphere of staff learner.

While in this camp the details of the first attack of the Somme Battle were told to all officers in lectures by the G.S.O.I. of the Division. Several days were employed burying cable in forward areas, and most officers were taken on 'Cook's Tours' up the line; this was a long dusty ride in a motor bus to Meaulte, then up to the high ground to the South with a map and a pair of field glasses to spy out the Promised Land. It was just as well that a kindly Providence hid us from what was in store for us on the green slopes beyond Fricourt and under the trees of the distant Delville Wood.

CHAPTER III

To the Battle of Arras

The battalion moved to a camp at Heilly on June 27th and remained there till the evening of the 30th when they marched to billets at Morlancourt. The original plan of the battle was that Fricourt should be pushed out by means of attacking divisions on either flank; the 50th Brigade were then to mop up Fricourt and to be followed in their advance by the 51st Brigade.

In the very early morning of July 1st, the last stores and bombs to be carried by the soldier were drawn from a dump, and everyone then prepared to move at a moment's notice. The hot day wore on through the morning and into the afternoon, and there was still no news of the capture of Fricourt. At last at 11.50 p.m. orders were received for the Brigade to move and replace the 50th Brigade in front of Fricourt, the 10th Sherwood Foresters to be in support to the 7th Lincolnshire Regt. and the 8th South Staffordshire Regt. On arrival in the forward area it was found that the 50th Brigade had suffered very heavily indeed, and had been unable to make any progress towards the village. Soon after daylight on the 2nd it was found that Fricourt had been evacuated by the enemy, and the advance was pushed slowly through Fricourt Wood. During the night of 2nd/3rd the 10th Sherwood Foresters reinforced the two forward battalions and good work was done by 'A' and 'D' companies and the bombers in clearing trenches north eastward from Fricourt wood towards Railway Alley and Crucifix Trench, (two strongly defended trenches running parallel to the enemy's front line). On the morning of July 3rd after an inconclusive attack on Railway Alley by the 7th Border Regt., 'C' and 'D' companies of the 10th Sherwood Foresters attacked the same trench with the 7th Lincolnshire Regt. This operation was completely successful, and pushing on towards Crucifix Trench and Railway Copse the companies captured about 800 prisoners of the 3rd Battn. 186th Regiment with the battalion commander. By the evening the battalion had consolidated a position along a well-marked hedge, about 1000 yards south-west of Contalmaison, stretching from Bottom Wood to Shelter Wood. Two field guns and four machine guns were captured, and casualties were comparatively light. It was in the capture of Railway Wood that an exploding bomb blinded Captain E. R. Oakden who unfortunately died as a result of the wound many months later.

July 4th was spent consolidating the positions gained, and that night the battalion was relieved by the 52nd Brigade and withdrawn to a canvas camp at Ville-sur-Ancre. A complete rest was tremendously enjoyed by everyone on the 5th and 6th Notes were compared about the battle, souvenirs were exhibited - 'pickelhaubes' galore, the Doctor's bitch which he 'captured' in a dugout at Fricourt, field glasses and revolvers. A few lucky people - wounded and at duty - interesting in bandages, came in for much attention. During the rest, Major G. D. Walker and Lieut. R. G. Milward were both seriously wounded while reconnoitring in the forward area.

But to return to the battle - the 52nd Brigade captured the next trench line (Quadrangle Trench) without much difficulty. They were, however, held up in Quadrangle Support Trench which lay in a hollow between Contalmaison and Mametz Wood, and which was badly enfiladed from both these positions. On July 7th the 52nd Brigade again attacked this trench without success. Early on that morning the 51st Brigade moved to the original British front line, prepared either to exploit success or to relieve the 52nd Brigade. From this position the battalion moved forward to Lone Copse, and thence two companies pushed on to Quadrangle Trench to relieve troops of the 52nd Brigade. The other two companies and Battn. H.Q. moved to the valley 400 yards north of Fricourt Wood. About 3 p.m. this valley was heavily shelled with 15cm. howitzers and many casualties occurred, amongst which were Major J. Hall-Brown and Capt. N. H. Pratt killed, and Lieut. W. H. Nelson died of wounds. Heavy rain fell most of the day and the enemy artillery fire was intense over the whole area. At 6.45 p.m. orders reached Battn. H.Q. at Railway Copse for an attack to be launched on Quadrangle Support at 8 p.m. This did not leave enough time for complete orders to reach all concerned; the attack, however, started to time but murderous enfilade fire from Contalmaison held up the troops in front of the objective, and they later withdrew to their starting point. During the night 7/8th the 7th Border Regt. relieved the 10th Sherwood Foresters who withdrew to the Northern Edge of Fricourt Wood. The battalion remained here till the evening of the 9th The 8th South Staffordshire Regt. attacked Quadrangle Support during the night 9/10th, and the 10th Sherwood Foresters pushed up 'A' and 'D' companies to hold Quadrangle Trench as it was vacated by the 8th South Staffs. This attack got right home but the whole position was made untenable owing to the same murderous enfilade fire from Contalmaison, and the South Staffordshire Regt. withdrew leaving the Sherwood Foresters and Lincolnshire Regt. to hold Quadrangle Trench. The remaining two companies were pushed forward to enable this to be done. During July 10th both Mametz Wood and Contalmaison were captured by British troops, and the enemy in his turn found that Quadrangle Support was untenable. Small groups of the enemy were seen to retire from this trench in the evening. Accordingly Lieut.-Col. Banbury, although expecting relief that night, ordered an attack to be made on Quadrangle Support at 9.45pm. The men, though dog-tired and muddy beyond description, pushed the attack well home and held their objective with little resistance. During the night 10/11th they were relieved by the 110th Brigade.

In the fighting from July 1st to the 11th the battalion had not, like so many others, been practically annihilated; it had, however, received many casualties, 15 officers and 366 other ranks; this included four captains and two majors. Capt. J. W. Fisher, D.S.O. was amongst these; he was hit during the attack on Quadrangle Support on the 7th and died at Heilly on the next day. He was so essentially one of the old battalion, and memories of Bovington and Lulworth all seem to include somewhere the cheeriness and good-tempered size of 'Fishcakes'. He had been wounded three times on previous dates. Capt. N. H. Pratt was another of the band of brothers who came out from England with the battalion. But the fighting had left the men hardened and determined with their 'tails well up'; the taking of the large number of prisoners on July 3rd and the ultimate capture of Quadrangle Support kept everyone's moral high. The position of Quadrangle Support was untenable as long as the enemy held Contalmaison. This fact was admitted by Staff Officers of the Division; the reasons for such a succession of isolated attacks upon it were two. First, the junction of the III and XIII Corps was immediately south of Contalmaison, so that simultaneous attacks held out no immediate prospect of success. This sounds so easy and such common-sense when it comes from the mouth of the Staff Officer, but the individual details of this policy of pitchforking troops at such positions are inevitably tragical and hideous.

As they trudged through Meaulte at dawn on July 11th, the battalion was more than a little sleepy, unshaven and muddy in the special and peculiar way that only the Somme can make a man muddy. There was, however, no lack of cheeriness, and breakfast eaten at the railway siding put a better aspect on life.

An empty ammunition train was allotted to the battalion; this eventually moved off at 3 p.m., and at 6 p.m. crawled into Saleux - south of Amiens. Orders had stated that the detraining place was Ailly-sur-Somme, and the R.T.O. at Saleux was very nice about it but 'this was where we had to detrain'! A certain number of motor buses had been collared by the pioneer battalion, so that all ranks including those wounded and at duty and those with sore feet were faced with a fourteen mile march to billets St. Pierre à Gouy, the village allotted to the battalion, was reached at 1.30 a.m. on July 12th, and we were able to make up arrears in sleep and to get a good wash during the next two days.

The chalet on the hill which was Battn. H.Q. was a wonderfully pleasant place with its deer on the lawn and the distant view of Amiens Cathedral; but after two days the rest area was changed and the battalion marched via Picquigny and Flixecourt to Ailly le Haut Clocher (known to the men as Ayley Lee Hort Closher). There we were able to get a real rest till July 23rd. There was very little ground available for training, and much time was needed to absorb all the reinforcements which arrived to make the Battalion up to strength Capt. C. J. A. Lefroy joined and took command of 'D' Company; 2nd Lieuts. C. F. S. Cox and R. S. Gustard also joined on the 17th and were with the battalion for a long time.

The policy of sending reinforcements up from the Base regardless of their regiment was first felt here; 230 other ranks of the South Staffordshire Regt. arrived for the battalion, and similar cases occurred through the division. Fortunately the system was only adopted during times of heavy casualties, but it always made for confusion and a certain amount of discontent.

The village was a comfortable one as regards billets, and some four miles away lay the cool sweet backwaters of the Somme which were delicious beyond all words to bathe in. Sudden orders to move were received on July 22nd; the first-line transport moved off early that morning; the rest of the battalion marched to Hangest, on the 23rd arriving there at 2 p.m. Six weary hours were spent waiting for a train, and at last at 8.40 p.m. we started for Mericourt. (The R. T. O. at Hangest during these six hours achieved the feat of being put under arrest more times than anyone else in the army during such a short time.) Detraining at Mericourt L'Abbaye, the battalion marched in the small hours of July 24th to bivouacs in a valley about one and a half miles north-east of the village. These were occupied until August 1st. The weather all this time was very fine and hot, and the men became adepts at erecting 'tamboos' each night with waterproof sheets. It was altogether a fine kind of life with frequent bathes in the Ancre close by. On July 26th Lieut.-Col. Banbury at length received well-deserved promotion to the rank of Brigadier-General, commanding the 61st Infantry Brigade. He had been in command of the battalion from the early days at Bovington. It is impossible to say how much the battalion owed to his sound military knowledge while training and his wise leadership in the field. During the ten days' fighting in July the success of the whole 51st Brigade was unquestionably due in no small measure to his initiative and his presence always in the most forward part of the battle.

Capt. L. Gilbert temporarily took command. On July 28th the entire infantry of the Division paraded in the vicinity of their bivouacs, and Major-General P. R. Robertson, C.B., C.M.G., presented several medal ribbons to officers and men who had been awarded them during the month

The Somme battle had made considerable progress since the battalion left the area on July 11th Bazentin le Petit, Bazentin le Grand, a part of High Wood, and Longueval had been captured. The 9th Division had fought their great fight, and Delville Wood had been lost and regained. Guillemont and the Sugar Factory between Guillemont and Longueval were still in the enemy's hands, leaving Delville Wood a pronounced salient.

On August 1st the 17th Division relieved the 21st Division who were holding from the N.E. corner of Delville Wood (right boundary) to the eastern outskirts of High Wood. The 51st Brigade was reserve Brigade, and the 10th Sherwood Foresters moved to the vicinity of Pommier Redoubt on the day of the divisional relief. The accommodation was a plain system of trenches on some rising ground from which a distant view of Delville wood was obtained. Bivouacs were soon made in the trenches and a few lucky people had Hun beds - low wooden things with criss-cross iron slates, a very doubtful luxury! The Somme 'chat' first introduced itself in wholesale quantities here; in the words of the immortal General Metcalfe: "This was no ordinary 'chat', for when challenged to mortal combat it did not scurry away or say 'kamerad', but it sat up on its little hind legs and barked defiance' ! A fearsome creature - it was rumoured that the Brigadier had more than a nodding acquaintance with them! On August 2nd 'Doc' Saunders the M.D. left the battalion to take command of an ambulance train. He was with the battalion during the early months in England: all

M.O.'s before Saunders were merely legendary. Everyone amongst the officers felt that he parted from a fine man, and in many cases a good friend. A few men who had tried the difficult path of the malingerer had cause to fear him, but to all ranks he was the 'good old Doc' in whose hands they would be as well cared for as possible in the R.A.P.

The 51st Brigade relieved the 52nd Brigade on the night 5/6th as right Brigade of the Division. The 10th Sherwood Foresters relieved the 9th Duke of Wellington's who were holding Longueval and the N.W. portion of Delville Wood. The conditions in this part of the line were as bad as any that were ever met with in France as regards stench, flies and filth The weather had been extraordinarily hot during all the fighting in the Wood, and as the enemy artillery were almost continuously active on the area, there had been no possibility of clearing the battlefield. Corpses in all stages of putrifaction were lying everywhere, and all day the sun blazed down and the flies grew fat and sleepy with the vile reek of the place.

Battalion Headquarters were first in Longueval, but after a direct hit had exploded a dump of bombs a few yards from the entrance, Headquarters were moved to a single shafted deep dugout on the southern outskirts of the wood; the entrance to the hole was in full view of the enemy in Guillemont. In the wood itself the positions held were merely a series of shell holes in the undergrowth; the digging of trenches was practically impossible owing to the tangled tree roots.

On August 6th some enemy posts were reported inside the wood on the front of the 7th Border Regiment on our immediate right. Delville Wood had been reported completely in our hands, and the discovery of these posts meant either they had been there all the time and had never been located, or else that the enemy had at some time made ground without interference from us. In either case the staff wanted to know Why? Who? When? Where? and that with the very utmost despatch. The 7th Border Regiment made several attacks on August 7th with the object of clearing the wood entirely, and the 10th Sherwood Foresters were ordered to conform with this advance. The attack was, however, unsuccessful, the only gain being the establishment of some advanced posts by the Sherwood Foresters. The chief defence of the enemy against these attacks appeared to be machine guns carefully concealed in some standing corn, and it was impossible to locate them. It was almost very difficult to get observed artillery fire on the foremost enemy positions; the only position of observation was from our own forward posts, and owing to the continuous shelling it was impossible to maintain communication with the batteries. It was certainly not for lack of trying, nor for lack of F.O.O.s in the front lines; the wires were just blown to shreds a few minutes after they were laid.

On the night 8th/9th the battalion was relieved by the 7th Lincolnshire Regt. and withdrew on relief to Montauban Alley, a trench on the southern side of Caterpillar Valley. Two worrying days in the vilest of places had made the men very tired. Many months afterwards I heard that from captured documents it was proved that the enemy posts had been established inside the edge of the wood several days before the 51st Brigade ever came into the line. The higher command at the time decided that it was the fault of the 51st Brigade that the enemy were inside the wood, and this resulted in a certain amount of recrimination and uneasiness. Lieut.-Col. R. J. Milne (Devon Regt.) took command of the battalion from August 10th; he had previously taken part in the capture of Montauban and Mametz by the 7th Division. On the same day the battalion were relieved by troops of the 52nd Brigade, and moved back to Pommiers Redoubt. Divisional relief took place on August 12th, and the battalion moved to the same bivouacs near Boire-sur-Ancre as they had occupied at the end of July. The Division was now transferred to the XVII Corps which was in the line opposite Gommecourt. The transport moved by road on the 14th and 15th, and the battalion entrained at Mericourt l'Abbaye in the afternoon of the 15th and detrained at Candas at 1 a.m. on the 16th From there an hour's march brought them to billets at Longuevillette. On the 17th a further move was made to Neuvellette (north of Doullens) where we remained till the 2th. On the 21st a long march after an early start brought us to St. Amand (east of Doullens) where we stayed as reserve troops till the 27th Billeting accommodation was good, and after the unending racket of Caterpillar Valley and Delville Wood it seemed after all that life might be worth living.

Capt. A. A. P. R. Stuart joined the battalion on the 21st with a host of other junior officers. On the 27th the battalion relieved the 7th Lincolnshire Regt. in the line between Fonquevillers and Hannescamps; owing to convenient orchards and deep trenches it was possible to carry out trench reliefs by daylight. The whole operation seemed to be absolutely playing at war; but this spot had seen some of the most determined fighting on July 1st when Gommecourt was attacked. Traces were still to be seen - No Man's Land was a mass of shallow assembly trenches, and the forward positions of the enemy showed signs of the tremendous bombardment to which they had been subjected. But there was practically no enemy activity, not even rifle fire, for No Man's Land was 1000 yards across. The 7th Lincolnshire Regt. had left an undesirable legacy - some gas cylinders installed in the front line, waiting for a favourable wind so that the stuff could be released. These furnished the only excitement worthy of mention;

no work or digging was allowed to take place near them, and an enormous amount of wires in code had to be sent about the creatures every day.

On August 29th Lieut. T. W. Daniel, M.C., rejoined the battalion after being wounded at the Bluff. This officer remained with the battalion until it was disbanded, and throughout the last great advance he commanded it.

The time from August 27th to Sept. 10th was employed in ordinary trench warfare of the dullest and most workaday type. On Sept. 10th the battalion was relieved by troops of the 33rd Division, and moved on that day and the next to Halloy immediately east of Doullens. Five days were spent in training for attacks, and on the 17th the battalion moved eastwards to Bayencourt. The 18th was spent with the whole battalion on working parties. On the 19th a long march was begun which lasted till the 24th, when the battalion arrived at Conteville (south of Auxi le Château), the route being via Doulens and Frohen le Petit. Training was carried out here till October 1st, though the cultivated land did not allow anything very extensive being done.

During this period Capt. G. J. Partridge - the adjutant, ('George Jimmy') left us for higher spheres; his name had been forwarded for the position of Brigade major in England, and he went to understudy the Brigade Major of the 51st Brigade. In a week's time he was in England. As the first adjutant that most of us ever knew his name is naturally very closely connected with all the doings of the battalion up to the date of leaving. As the smoother of the paths of newly arrived subalterns in England, as the owner of a gently deprecating voice at the end of the telephone at X a.m. (where X is some very small number), as an intensely human man and yet at the same time an efficient adjutant, as the proud possessor of all these virtues - and more, he will be for ever remembered by those who know him.

Lieut. F. C. Hodder took over the duties of adjutant. Orders to move came suddenly on the night of Sept. 30th; the O.C. 'C' company (Capt. Daniel) was celebrating his twenty-first birthday; nearly all Headquarters and the company officers were there and they started a concert. Just as things were working to a climax at 2 a.m. a sleepy runner arrived with orders to move by march route at 6 a.m. to Halloy! A further move to Bayencourt was made the next day, and on October 6th the Battn. relieved the 7th Border Regt. in trenches east of Hebuterne. The object of all the moving backwards and forwards from Sept. 15th onwards appeared to be that the higher command expected the battle of the Somme, raging a few miles to the south, to develop northwards; by striking north from the region of the Butte de Warlencourt the enemy at Gommecourt and Puisieux might be so threatened in the rear as to force him to retire. Whenever there appeared a likelihood of this occurring, all available divisions in the VII Corps had to be in a state of readiness; but when the battle in the south appeared to be stagnant, as many divisions as possible were given training opportunities. On arrival at Bayencourt on October 2nd we found arrangements going forward at the very highest pressure for a great advance on the Gommecourt front. Howitzer batteries sprang up like mushrooms in the night all round Sailly au Bois; enormous dumps of bombs, S. A. A., Very Lights etc. were made in the trenches, and carrying parties were incessant for the formation of these dumps. The artillery started cutting wire on the enemy front, and tank tracks were made. Pages and pages of instructions were vomited forth by Brigade H.Q. all for 'Zero' Day. But 'Zero' Day never came - on October 9th the whole scheme was abandoned; the heavy batteries disappeared even as quickly as they had come; and on October 10th the battalion was relieved by troops of the 33rd Division and concentrated at Bayencourt. They remained at Bayencourt till the 19th when a move was made by march route to Lucheux. From here the 17th Division was transferred to the XIV Corps commanded by General the Earl of Cavan, which was fighting in the southern portion of the British front on the Somme battlefield. Since the 17th Division left the Somme in August the line had swept forward with the advance of the tanks, and now heavy howitzers were tucked away in the chaos of Delville Wood, and Flers - Morval - and Guedecourt were in our hands.

The first line transport moved south in a two-day journey starting on the 21st, and the battalion followed in buses on the 22nd, de-bussing at Mericourt l'Abbaye. The bus ride was made on a very cold day and was most uncomfortable.

Billets were occupied in Mericourt until the 26th, when a move was made to the Citadel Camp south of Fricourt; thence on the 29th to a camp immediately east of Montauban, and on the next day October 30th relieved troops of the 8th Division in the line facing Le Transloy.

On the way up the line something was seen of the conditions which were going to be faced for the most part of the winter. Heavy rain had fallen recently without any sun following to dry the ground. The main road through Mametz and Montauban, up which all the supplies of a large part of the front had to travel, was in an appalling state; it never appeared to have been properly mended since its capture in July and now the whole of the metalled surface was a mass of pasty gravel, churned into ruts sometimes a couple of feet deep, while the wheels of the transport rested on the slimy chalk underneath Farther forward there were merely trackless deserts of the altogether indescribable Somme mud. A straggling line of duckboards went forward from Waterlot Farm, near Guillemont; some of these were floating, some tipped on one side , some just upset the unwary walker for no apparent reason. After about a mile of these boards on which one performed feats worthy of Blondin, they ceased, and one pushed out into the void at the mercy of a 'guide'.

Ian Hay in the 'First Hundred Thousand' never said a truer thing than when he remarked that there were only two types of guides - those who don't know the way and confess it, and those who don't know the way and keep the fact a secret.

Both types of guides were met with on the night of relief, but somehow everyone eventually fetched up and after starting from Montauban at 3 p.m. on October 30th relief was reported complete at 7 a.m. on the following morning. When the trenches were actually reached they exceeded even the worst fears of the company pessimist. Log after, when discussing trenches and trench mud with Capt. E. B. Joyce and others, they all agreed that the conditions in this sector were really the worst that they had ever experienced. Mud up to your middle and deeper, with no bottom to the stuff if anyone optimistically began shovelling it away. Naturally in such conditions troops could only be a very short time in the line; but this cut both ways, for it meant a correspondingly short time in the camp in rear. The usual thing was 48 hours in the front line, 24 hours in a reserve position some 2000 yards in rear, 48 hours in a camp near Montauban, then 24 hours in the reserve position before going into the line again. The enemy artillery added to the general hellishness of the situation. The Hun knew where all the deep dugouts were, and he never seemed to grow weary of shelling them. The sunken road, running parallel to the line where the Battn. H.Q. were established was a perpetual target; and one of the standing fatigues for the H.Q. servants was to crawl out about an hour after dawn and fill in the shell holes which had been made during the night over the officers' dugout. The exact position of the trenches occupied is difficult to describe, and still more difficult to recognise on the ground, a thing which we tried to do in August 1918. The enemy front trench (Zenith Trench) overlooked a considerable part of our line (Misty and Gusty Trenches), and the 8th Division had made several unsuccessful attempts to capture it.

Running eastwards from Zenith Trench was a straight communication trench (Eclipse Trench). The battalion was relieved by the 7th Border Regt. on the night of November 1/2nd, and withdrew to the vicinity of Montauban. The Lincolnshire Regt. and the Border Regt. cleverly captured Zenith Trench with little or no artillery resistance.

About this time Lieut.-Col. Milne was sent to command the Divisional and later the Corps School at Daours near Amiens, and did not return till May 1917. Major L. Gilbert assumed command of the battalion.

On the evening of November 5th the battalion moved to the support positions, relieving the Lincolnshire Regt. The Hun unconsciously celebrated Guy Fawkes Day by putting up the most extraordinary number of coloured Very Lights without any apparent reason. On the night November 6/7th the battalion relieved the 8th South Staffordshire Regt. in the line. The same night Capt. T. W. Daniel, with a small party of men, drove the enemy out of some old gunpits about 80 yards from our front line; the pits were then linked up to our trench. During the following night a bombing party advanced about 350 yards eastwards along Eclipse Trench with little resistance; a stop was established and a trench was then dug running north-eastwards from the stop to our front line. These advances, though small, denied observation to the enemy, and were made in such appalling conditions that they were really very fine performances.

The 7th Border Regt. relieved the battalion on the night of the 8th/9th, and the latter took up the position of support, going back to Montauban the next evening. Divisional relief came on November 11th when the battalion marched to the vicinity of Meaulte, thence they entrained at Edgehill for Hangest (still with the same truculent R.T.O!)

One night was spent in billets at Hangest and Le Quesnoy, and on the next day the battalion moved to Picquigny where they stayed till December 12th A considerable amount of training was done while here - particularly musketry, and company commanders got a much needed chance to know their men. The work was always light, and everyone tried hard to remember as little as possible of the horror of the slough from which they had come. The village itself was comfortable, and the people were in many cases more than friendly. Marching through the same place two years later, a few of the men who still survived recognised their old friends. Amiens was not very far away, some 18 kilometres, and ever since July 1916 that city played its part nobly in making the toils of the battle seem lighter and a little further off than they would have been otherwise. It was known that Christmas Day would be spent in all probability in intense discomfort in the forward area, so December 10th was chosen for the day on which Christmas Dinners were to be eaten. After a great deal of bartering and babbling three pigs and much beer were bought. The pigs were roasted in the local bakery and eaten with huge gusto by the men at midday. They drowsed off the effects in the afternoon. In the evening all the officers had dinner in Battn. H.Q. Mess. This was a very cheery show; Lieut.-Col. Milne presided; drinks were many and various, and a certain young subaltern learnt that champagne and chartreuse must not be mixed under any circumstances. Lieuts. Jacques and Nevitt formed the backbone of the football team which specially distinguished itself during the rest.

The battalion moved by train to Corbie on December 12th; the transport as usual made a two-day journey of it by road. Further training in musketry was carried out here. The 17th Division were lucky to be in General Cavan's Corps, and while at Corbie he lectured to all the officers. He seemed to be, more than any other General of similar rank, so thoroughly human and appreciative of the point of view of the poor wretch in the front line.

The Prince of Wales was attached to the Corps Staff, and in the following months he was often seen on the duckboards in the forward area, followed by a staff officer who always looked extremely anxious both for his own and the Prince's safety.

On December 23rd a move was made to Mericourt l'Abbaye, and then on the next day to a hutted camp on the Carnoy-Montauban road. This move was part of the relief of the 20th Division by the 17th Division. The 20th Division were in the line east of Les Boeufs, immediately to the south of the front which the 10th Sherwood Foresters held in the first part of November. The positions of the front lines had not altered since that date as the weather had entirely put a stop to any active operations on a large scale. The chief changes in the forward area were two: the lessening of the artillery fire on both sides, and the improvement of communication. Miles of duckboard tracks raised on piles had been laid; pack horses no longer floundered through mud up to their bellies, each laden with six 18 pdr. shells; these now came up by Decauville Railway. In the very forward area conditions had not altered much, but the men moved about in the trenches as little as possible and kept the few square feet where they spent the 48 hours or so as dry as possible by means of dams and mud scoops. Thigh gumboots again had to be worn which resulted in a large number of sores, and in some cases trench feet. During this tour in the same the Divisional Commander divided the twelve infantry battalions into two Brigade groups, and the line was held by these two groups - each holding half of the divisional front. Two battalions of each group were in the front line at the same time for a tour of 48 hours; on relief they marched back to a hutted camp on the Carnoy-Montauban road where they remained for three days; then they moved for 24 hours to iron shelters at Guillemont and into the front line on the following night. This group system was used so that each Brigade H.Q. in turn might get a rest in a hutted camp; the H.Q. of the Brigades in the line were at Guillemont where the conditions made a prolonged stay a most undesirable thing.

At Carnoy the battalion came under the orders of the G.O.C. 52nd Brigade. It was here that Capt. J. N. Knight rejoined us after his wound at Poperinghe; he remained in command of 'A' company until he was gassed in August 1918. Christmas Day passed practically unnoticed; the Nissen huts at Carnoy never did inspire one to celebrate anything in particular, least of all Christmas.

On December 26th the battalion moved to the iron shelters at Guillemont, donned their gum boots thigh, picked up 48 hours' rations, and started off on the following afternoon to relieve the 12th Manchester Regt. No offensive operations were contemplated, so only 400 men were taken into the line with the battalion; the remainder were taken to form sapping platoons under Brigade supervision or road mending companies under Divisional orders.

The distribution of troops was very much in depth; the whole battalion had spread out on a front of 400 yards to a depth of a mile. Shelling of the support line, Antelope Trench, was rather heavy during the tour but otherwise nothing noteworthy occurred. On the night of December 30/31st the battalion was relieved by the 9th Duke of Wellington's, and withdrew to Carnoy camp. The Division remained in the line till January 11th, during which time the battalion was in the front line from Jan. 3rd to 5th and 8th to 11th Both tours were uneventful; conditions became better in the front trenches, and the long gum boots were only worn by men moving between the forward posts, otherwise they wore ordinary ankle boots and puttees and used a good deal of anti-frostbite grease.

From Carnoy on January 13th the battalion marched to Meaulte, and remained there resting and training till the 26th The accommodation was very rough and the troops did not get the complete rest which the stay at Picquigny gave. The 'Derby' recruits had already begun to arrive in the battalion, and 200 of these were sent off to a musketry camp at Pontremy to undergo further training.

The 17th Division again relieved the 20th Division on January 27th This division was holding the southern portion of the front held by the XIV Corps, from immediately north of Sailly Saillisel (northern boundary) to Rancourt (a village facing St. Pierre Vaast Wood). This tour in the line was the least uncomfortable of all in the Somme area, being chiefly due to the immensely hard frost which lasted almost the whole tour; mud and water disappeared, the ground became like iron, and all the shell holes were frozen over with ice inches thick. A biting east wind blew most of the time and conditions seemed to be arctic, but this was a thousand times better than the sickening mud and driving rain which we had experienced in November.

The twelve infantry battalions were again divided into two Brigade groups, and the method of holding the line was very much as before. Each battalion was usually two days (sometimes four) in the front line; on relief they marched to Maltzhorn Camp, a wretched collection of tents south of Trones Wood; the next day they moved further back to huts at Bronfay Farm. After two days here they moved to a support position between Bouleaux Wood and Morval, and waited there 24 hours before going into the line once more. The frost made trench life totally different from what it had ever been before. Digging was almost out of the question; pickaxes were blunted or broken by the dozen on the hard surface; the churned-up state of the ground enabled the frost to penetrate deeper than it would otherwise have done. There was a light powdering of snow on the ground, and any patrol wishing to approach the enemy front line had to wear white overalls. Watercarts used to arrive at Haie Wood (midway between Combles and Sailly Saillisel) frozen hard; a long suffering dump guard would then crawl forth from a dugout, and try to persuade a sandbag and a few chips to burn underneath the frozen taps until they were thawed. No sooner was the water in petrol cans ready to be taken up the line than it froze again, and the same process had to be repeated when it arrived at the front trenches. But all discomforts were swamped by the joy of walking dry shod over the ground where before one had slithered and floundered in seas of mud.

The battalion was in the front line from January 28th to 30th, from February 3rd to the 5th, from the 9th to the 13th, and again from the 17th to the 19th At about 5.30 p.m. on February 5th the enemy attempted a small raid on the battalion. The party of about 20 men crept up dressed in white suits and jumped into the front trench between our extreme right hand post and the extreme left hand post of the South Staffordshire Regt. The distance between these posts was 80 yards. A few well thrown bombs sent the enemy back over No Man's Land considerably quicker than he came. Several were killed and one wounded prisoner of the 120th R.I.R. was left in our hands. Two men of 'A' company were missing. Nothing else worthy of note occurred during the other tours in the line.

Divisional relief came on the 19th, and the battalion entrained at the Plateau, detrained at Heilly, and marched to Bonnay, a village between Heilly and Corbie.

Rumour had it that the Division was going to be transferred to the Fifth Army to help in the fighting which had been going on fairly continuously in the Ancre Valley. But after a few days at Bonnay the great German Retreat began and the whole Somme battlefield became a deserted waste with the firing line some miles to the east of it. The troops of the XIV Corps which were then in the line remained to follow up the retreating enemy, and the 17th Division was placed in G.H.Q. Reserve. An almost continuous series of moves was now started which culminated in the battle of Arras, and therefore little serious training could be done. The battalion moved to Herissart on March 2nd, thence to Le Quesnoy - south of Hesdin. March 22nd and 23rd were taken up with moving by march route to Le Souich, a few miles north of Doullens, halting for one night at Rougefay. Training was continued here, and on several occasions the battalion was used for road mending purposes. The main Doullens - St. Pol road was on many days a solid mass of howitzers of all calibres going northwards from the Somme area, and although labour battalions were at work on the roads they could not keep pace with the damage done on the surface.

Le Souich is a place of pleasant memories. The instruments for the band arrived here. Most of the musicians belonging to a disbanded battalion at home had arrived some time before as reinforcements. They had been carefully camouflaged 'en bloc' , and needed little training before they blared forth tuneful noises. Nodder came into his own as a bandmaster, and in a few hours' time he was prancing up and down the village street at the head of a band which might have been mistaken for the Coldstream Guards at a little distance.

There was a football match; the officers of the battalion versus the officers of the 7th Lincolnshire Regt. I forget the score, but the match, although played in a snowstorm, was a good one.

A battalion dinner for the officers followed this, the second and last which was ever held in France. The speeches at the end included a slightly sensational account of the football match compiles by Schomberg the padre. There is no record of the exact date when Schomberg joined the battalion (it was sometime in March) or when he left, but during his stay he made himself felt as a moving spirit in all the battalion activities, and did his duty nobly in a way which was thoroughly appreciated by all ranks. He was invariably cheery, with a keen wit; the regimental canteen was his particular forte, and the way in which he maintained adequate stocks in the canteen and brought it along to the forward area in a surplus vehicle and with the aid of his well-known grey horse, was a model to all such institutions and padres.

Capt. W. E. Brandt joined the battalion at the close of the dinner, and was hailed loudly by his old friends whom he knew in England; he remained with the battalion until just before the Armistice. Capt. J. A. Meads, M.C. who had been wounded at the Bluff rejoined here.

CHAPTER IV
Arras and Ypres 1917

While at Le Souich the general plans of the battle of Arras were sketched out in lectures to all officers by the G.S.O.I. of the Division. For the beginning of this battle the 17th Division was attached to the Cavalry Corps. The infantry were to break through the German defensive system; the cavalry were then to follow up the success. The 17th Division were to follow as quickly as possible and relieve the Cavalry in the positions they had taken up, to allow the latter to push on still further. The general direction of advance was to be eastwards from Arras down the Arras-Cambrai road. The great defensive systems round Vitry en Artois and Boiry Notre Dame, which afterwards became the famous Drocourt-Queant line, were then far from complete, so that once the cavalry were clear of Monchy there would be no organised defences in front of them.

For the division to fulfil its rôle, speed in marching was essential; much attention was given to route marches and feet hardening; the equipment to be carried by all ranks was also cut down to the absolute minimum. The battalion left Le Souich on April 6th and began a three days' march which eventually brought them to their jumping off area; Habacq - a village south of the Arras - St. Pol road, and about 5 miles from Arras. Nights were spent in Maisnil - St. Pol and Ambrines. None of the marches were long; the weather was good, and it helped to harden the mens' feet. April 8th (Easter Sunday) was a particularly fine day, warm and calm. In the forward area everyone seemed to be absolutely on their toes waiting for the word to go, and the weather seemed as though it was settled for a long fine spell. But as everyone knows, the weather played into the hands of the enemy. At zero hour - 5.30 a.m. - there was a furious westerly gale with occasional sleet showers. A long day of waiting started; news came through slowly; it was good but there was no mention of a complete breakthrough.

In anticipation of further success the three brigades of the 17th Division were moved eastwards along the roads on which they were to march according to plan. The 10th Sherwood Foresters moved northwards late in the afternoon to the Arras - St Pol road, thence along this road towards Arras. The road was fearfully congested with traffic, armoured cars, endless motor ambulances, a batch a prisoners under a mounted escort, ammunition wagons pushing and hurrying their way along; a large cage packed with newly captured Huns was a very cheering sight with a little fiery A.P.M. stalking up and down in front like a lion tamer.

The weather now became cloudy and snow began to fall lightly. Halts in the column became more and more frequent until finally when 2 miles west of Arras we received orders to bivouac for the night in a field by the roadside. By this time it was snowing in good earnest, and the discomfort of the night can be well imagined. The Cavalry who had spent most of the day on the eastern outskirts of Arras came back to bivouac on the opposite side of the road. They had not had a chance to get into action, but their opportunity came the next day; some had breakfast with us and then moved forward to their bloody fight near Monchy where they suffered so heavily. The failure to continue the initial success of the attack became more and more apparent, so that the chances of the Division Fulfilling the rôle allotted to it became very small.

Early in the morning of April 10th the battalion marched into billets in Arras; vacant cellars and rooms were available on all sides; we settled down to wait for orders - meanwhile making ourselves as comfortable as possible. Three days were spent thus waiting, while the fighting round Monchy became more and more intense. At last on the 12th the 17th Division was transferred to the VI Corps who were fighting on a front from Monchy inclusive northwards to the Scarpe. On this date the battalion moved to the Railway Triangle, a large strong point which had lain some 1000 yards behind the original German line. The weather still continued to be wretched with frequent snow showers, but there was fairly good accommodation as the place had been a dump for R.E. material for the enemy; shelters were quickly erected. The whole 51st Brigade concentrated in this area; they were reserve Brigade of the Division which was now holding a front on the south bank of the Scarpe. Our advance here had penetrated the last organised defence of the enemy, but it was unable to make further headway; local fighting for small tactical features took place, but the enemy had built up a defence of machine guns disposed in great depth; he also employed crossfire from the northern bank of the Scarpe to a large extent so that the only prospect of success seemed to lie in a concerted advance along both banks of the river after heavy artillery preparation. The necessary artillery for this was slow in coming up owing to the incessantly bad weather, and the date of this attack was not until the 23rd.

On April 14th the battalion relieved troops of the 52nd Brigade, the support Brigade, in the Brown Line, an enemy system of trenches about 1000 yards west of our new front line; the shelling on this line was very heavy at intervals. By night the battalion was employed in digging assembly trenches on the divisional front preparatory to the big attack, and one night was spent in clearing the streets of Monchy which were blocked by carcasses of horses. On April 18th the whole Brigade moved back to the Railway Triangle so as to be rested and fit for the 23rd. Detailed orders were received here for the big attack. The 51st Brigade were to be the assaulting Brigade on a two battalion front; the 7th Border Regt. were to be the right leading battalion and were to be followed by the 10th Sherwood Foresters. This battalion was then to pass through the Border Regt. if the attack progressed well after reaching a certain line. On April 21st the battalion again moved into the brown Line, and thence on the night 22/23rd into their jumping-off trenches - some 800 yards behind the leading battalion.

The only outstanding enemy defence was Bayonet Trench, a narrow rough trench running north and south along the whole Brigade front, forming the enemy front line; also Rifle Trench running roughly at right angles to it. The junction of Bayonet and Rifle trenches was approximately opposite the inter-battalion boundary of the 51st Brigade. Zero hour was 4.50 a.m. It was a very clear and cloudless night, and at zero it was quite light enough to see down the sights of a machine gun.

The enemy barrage in reply to our bombardment came down about 200 yards behind our front line, and by the time the 10th Sherwood Foresters had advanced 500 yards they were in the middle of severe shelling which caused many casualties. Before reaching Bayonet Trench it was apparent that the attack was not progressing satisfactorily, for heavy machine gun fire from the north was encountered; the extreme left of the battalion were obliged to go to ground in shell holes; the majority, however, on the right reached Bayonet Trench. At this time Lieut.-Col. Gilbert, who was in command of the battalion, was moving forward to a new position but lost direction, and entered a part of Bayonet Trench which was still in the hands of the enemy; he was wounded and taken prisoner. Capt. T. W. Daniel then assumed command. He found that the Border Regt. had been able to make but little headway; their leading companies had crossed Bayonet Trench but had suffered very severe casualties from machine gun fire from Rifle Trench and its vicinity, and were unable to advance further. The 8th South Staffordshire Regt. on the left flank had been unable to reach Bayonet Trench at any point north of its junction with Rifle Trench; heavy machine gun fire from the Scarpe marches and the north bank of the river stopped their advance. The attack north of the Scarpe also was quickly held up; the 51st Division there encountered very strong resistance in Roeux which they were unable to capture completely. 2nd Lieut. Bowmer won the Military Cross by leading a bombing attack which gained 150 yards of Bayonet Trench.

It was some hours before the situation became clear, and all the time artillery officers had their eyes glued to their glasses in the O.P.s trying to locate the enemy machine guns which were doing the damage, but without result. Capt. Daniel advocated a bombing attack down Bayonet Trench, and a supply of bombs was sent up for that purpose; the Division, however, forbade that form of attack and decided to launch the 50th Brigade against Bayonet and Rifle Trenches after further artillery preparation. This attack was held up in exactly the same way as that of the 51st Brigade early in the morning. In the small hours of April 24th troops of the 50th Brigade relieved the 10th Sherwood Foresters who withdrew to the Railway Triangle. Officer casualties had been heavy out of all proportion to those suffered by the men. Lieut. W. R. L. Davis was killed; he was an old original 10th Battalion officer who joined as a reinforcement. Capt. J. P. Tucker, 2nd Lieuts. J. P. McCombe and G. R. Y. Thurlow were also killed; these were all good men whose loss the battalion felt keenly.

The only thing which had held up the advance on the 23rd was the great depth in which the German machine guns were distributed, and the tenacity of the men behind these guns. On the night of the 24/25th the whole of Bayonet Trench and Rifle Trench was captured by the 52nd Brigade; the haul of prisoners was small but they all stated that they had definite orders to hold on to the very last.

Capt. T. W. Daniel, M.C., was awarded the D.S.O. for this action.

On April 25th the battalion marched to Arras where they entrained; they detrained at Saulty and marched to billets in Grand Rullecourt. Five days were spent here in much needed rest and reorganisation. Lieut.-Col. R. J. Milne rejoined here and took command.

The 17th Division was transferred to XVII Corp, holding a front from the Scarpe to Gavrelle. Another attack on a large scale was planned for May 3rd; the division was, however, only to come into action if the advance was thoroughly successful, and were to be in a position of readiness shortly after zero.

A long dusty move was made by motor bus to a hutted camp ('Y' huts) on the St. Pol - Arras road west of Etrun on May 1st. Early on the 3rd the battalion marched to bivouacs on the eastern outskirts of Arràs, close to the candle factory.

The attack by troops in the line met with little better success than on April 23rd. After this unsuccessful operation the higher command apparently gave up all idea of driving the enemy further eastwards on this particular front by means of large attacks, and a long period of trench warfare started.

For a week the battalion remained at the candle factory. Corps signals conceived the idea of an extensive system of buried cable and the battalion was used for this work while they were in this camp. Burying cable is an unsatisfactory job for Thomas Atkins; the work is not like digging an ordinary trench which is obviously some good and along which he will probably walk some day with a feeling of security; but he digs a trench much deeper and narrower than usual, in this case down into hard chalk, and then after all his labour the officer tells him to fill it in again!

The 17th Division took over a front extending from immediately south of Gravelle to a point about 200 yards north of the Arras - Vitry Railway on May 10th. The 10th Sherwood Foresters moved to the deep railway cutting in the Arras - Lens railway north of the Arras - Gravelle road. On the 12th May they moved forward into the old German defensive system running north and south from the western outskirts of Fampoux, the Green Line; here they came under the orders of the 50th Brigade who were considerably exhausted by some intense local fighting. For two days the companies were used to the utmost of their capacity in carrying stores and ammunition for the Brigade, and the men were far from fresh when they relieved the 10th West Yorkshire Regt. (50th Brigade) in the line on the night 14/15th The front line was then Cuba Trench, immediately east of the Roeux - Gravelle road. A complicated relief was taking place on the right flank of the battalion on the same night; the division on the right was extending their front and taking over more line from the 17th Division. At dawn the enemy launched an attack to the right of the 10th Sherwood

Foresters. The relief in this part was still incomplete and a certain amount of confusion was caused. The enemy, however, did not push home the attack with great vigour, and by noon our front line was re-established. No attack took place on the front of the 10th Sherwood Foresters, but the right support company formed a defensive flank and did a certain amount of bombing down the trenches; but the enemy did not seem inclined to stay and fight it out, and he quickly retired leaving several prisoners. A great deal of shelling was directed on this sector, but there were few casualties owing to the trenches being well dug. The battalion remained in the line until May 20th when they were relieved by troops of the 50th Brigade. The only excitement during this tour was the bringing down of an enemy aeroplane just outside the parapet on our front line on the 18th Low flying planes had annoyed us constantly, particularly at dawn. This time a great volume of Lewis gun fire was brought to bear on the Hun and he made a forced landing. Both pilot and observer were taken prisoner. Maps and instruments were also 'souvenired' from the machine, but the ever watchful intelligence officer demanded all of these that he could trace.

After relief on the night May 20/21st the battle withdrew to the camps close to the candle factory known as St. Nicholas Camp. On the 22nd they were ordered to bivouac in the old German support line, about 400 yards west of the deep railway cutting mentioned before. From here they were employed every night in cable burying in the forward area which was under direct observation of the enemy, so the work had to be done at night. It was wearisome work, but the men worked with a will, and earned high praise from the Corps Signals. On the afternoon of the 26th the enemy shelled the bivouacs with a high velocity gun. On a clear day the enemy were able to get a remarkably clear view of the north side of the Scarpe valley from Jigsaw Wood, and on several occasions he used his high velocity gun with very frightening effect. The shells themselves seemed to go so deep into the ground that there was no shrapnel effect and little damage was done, but the sudden 'swish bang' of the heavy shell is most disconcerting to say the least of it. Capt. T. H. Willcox was unlucky enough to lose half an ear from a bit of one of these shells.

On May 27th the battalion moved to the Green Line as support to the 51st Brigade; they remained here till relieved on the night 30/31st by troops of the 101st Brigade 33rd Division. On relief the battalion went from Arras by train to Mondicourt on the Arras-Doullens road, where they were billetted. Three weeks of much needed training were put in here; for a period of almost twelve months they had been unable to settle down to any progressive training; during all the other long periods out of the line they had seldom stayed more than a week in the same place, and all the time seemed to have been employed in moving and reconnoitring training facilities. This time the areas were good; Brigade field days were arranged and all ranks benefited largely. A Divisional Horse Show was held on June 7th Doullens was not so very far away, so that a lorry jump or a ride on the Company Commander's nag ensured a cheery meal at the Quatre Fils d'Aymon or the Bonne Aire.

The 51st Brigade returned to Arras by buses on June 21st, and the battalion once more found themselves in St. Nicholas Camp. Three nights here were spent on the old job of cable burying. Orders were then received that the 17th Division was taking over approximately the same front as before on June 3th. While holding this part of the line the 33rd Division had advanced the whole front some 200 yards, and by means of this advance the enemy were denied much observation of our front trench system. Roeux and the Chemical Works had also been captured by British troops. The situation generally was very quiet on the front, so that the Division held more line than before; the northern boundary was as before (south of Gravelle) but the southern boundary ran along the northern outskirts of Roeux, and the Division was responsible for the Chemical Works and the Arras-Vitry Railway. The 10th Sherwood Foresters relieved troops of the 33rd Division in the extreme left sector on the night 29/3th. One company of the 3/4th West Kent Regt. was attached to the battalion for instruction in trench warfare during this tour in the line; this regiment replaced the 9th Northumberland Fusiliers who left the 17th Division and were amalgamated with the other battalions of the 34th Division. The 17th Division held this front until September 23rd. Two Brigades were in the front line at a time - each with two battalions in the front line and two in support; the third Brigade rested in St. Nicholas Camp. Each Brigade was 16 days in the line, and 8 at rest, so that for the battalions it worked out at 8 days in camp, 8 days in support, and 8 days in the front line. Lieut. Reynard joined the battalion early in July from the South Notts. Hussars and was appointed Transport Officer.

It was a pleasant enough life on the whole; in the front line there was a certain amount of trench mortar activity which gave great annoyance at times. The aeroplane photo experts made sure that at one time they had spotted the emplacements of a pair of these 'minnies', and a special raid was made to wipe them out. But the raiding party on arrival only found a couple of thoroughly well-used Hun latrines!

A distinct feature of the enemy forward area was that very little work was done in it. The trenches that were dug were of the roughest and sketchiest description, and the Hun never dug a regular traversed front, support, and reserve line such as those that faced us at the beginning of the Somme battle. Practically all the enemy's digging and wiring activities were concentrated on the Drocourt - Queant line which on this front passed immediately west of Vitry-en-Artois, some three miles east of his front line. It was thought by the higher command that this lack of activity in the forward area meant that the enemy intended to withdraw some day, probably in the autumn. Detailed schemes for following up this retirement were planned out by all formations which never took place.

An immense amount of R.E. work was done on the trenches in this area. A system of localities and strong points was planned out, and gradually completed for all-round defence, and a deep dugout was constructed in each strong point. Long communication trenches made approach to the front line possible without coming under enemy observation. These trenches were all fitted with duckboards, A. frames, and revetting, so that by the end of September the place was altogether a show sector.

The enemy activity with artillery became very slight, and the monotony was relieved one day by a visit from Mr. Horatio Bottomley; armed with a tin hat, box respirator, and a secretary; he was taken up to the Green Line - some 800 yards behind the front line; here he was allowed to look over the parapet. He arrived just in time to see one of our planes crash from a direct hit with an 'archie'. Next week the two middle pages of Mr. Bottomley's periodical were full of the visit to the 'hell' and of the people he met there. It seems a pity that such a man was not allowed to go to a really hot place, not to Hell, but to a place where fighting and offensive operations were in progress; the impact of his after writings would strike a much truer note than it did in this case. Certain events which concerned the battalion while in this sector must be mentioned, as being of outstanding importance.

On July 22nd the battalion was in St. Nicholas camp. The Hun had evidently brought up a new long range gun, 24cm - naval type; he was able to see the tops of some of the tents from Jigsaw Wood, and started slowly bombarding them. The first shell carried away half the Brigadier's hut about 100 yards from the camp. Fortunately he happened to be in the other half of the hut and he strolled out of this looking only a trifle surprised, through the smoke and wreckage! Divisional Headquarters close by received the next few shells. After about an hour's pause two shells pitched right into the battalion camp just as the men were turning out for church parade; one shell narrowly missed the entire band, but by some miracle no casualties at all occurred. The camp was quickly evacuated and the battalion accommodated elsewhere. This same gun was quiet from that time onwards until the day of divisional relief when the transport of the incoming division got a warm reception.

On August 8th the battalion was in the line south of the Arras - Vitry Railway. At 3.45am. the enemy attempted a raid at approximately the boundary between the Sherwood Foresters and the Lincolnshire Regt. Special 'sturm truppe' were employed for the purpose, but the party were beaten off with heavy loss before they reached our front line, leaving one wounded prisoner in our hands. The enemy were so furious at the failure of the raid that a party of nine again attempted to reach our lines about noon on the same day. Some long sap heads ran out into No Man's Land from the front line held by the battalion. A sentry saw the Germans outside one of these sap heads and gave the alarm. 2nd Lieut. W. C. Wicks at once ran out with four men. They were greeted by a shower of bombs which wounded three men. Wicks and the one remaining man then charged the enemy and killed four of them; Wicks shooting three with his revolver; the rest of the enemy ran back to their own lines. 2nd Lieut. Wicks received the Military Cross as an immediate award for his gallant conduct.

On August 11th Lieut.-Col. R. J. Milne went to be Second in Command of the 7th Somerset Light Infantry; Lieut.-Col. H. J. King of the K.O.Y.L.I. arrived to take command.

On August 20th Major A.A.P.R. Stuart was evacuated to England sick, and Major T.W. Daniel was appointed Second in Command of the battalion. A raid on a fairly large scale was carried out by troops of the 10th Sherwood Foresters on the night of September 16/17th The selected troops - 3 officers and 35 men - were kept out of the line for a fortnight and practised their task over trenches which were marked out to resemble the actual ones. The raiders went over in three parties, got through the wire and well amongst the Boches. Many of the enemy were killed and at least six dugouts were destroyed with Stokes Mortar bombs. Only one prisoner was brought back; he was the regimental postman who was actually delivering letters when captured; and his mailbag afforded valuable information. 2nd Lieut. Wicks was unfortunately killed, and Lieuts. F.B. Joyce and C.F.S. Cox both received the Military Cross for gallantry. On Sept. 23rd the 61st Division relieved the 17th Division. It was an open secret that the Division was to go up north and take part in the heavy fighting east of Ypres. Those of us who knew the Salient had followed closely the course of the fighting which began on July 31st, and we had also watched with very mingled feelings one division after another go from the comparatively peaceful Third Army sector to the Second and Fifth Armies in Belgium. We had heard grisly tales from some of these divisions who had been sent down south again exhausted, and the thought of fighting up there in October gave those of us who knew the country a cold grey feeling inside.

After a two-day march the battalion arrived at Grand Rullecourt on September 26th. Five days were spent here training. Special attention was paid to advancing against 'pill boxes'. These buildings of various sizes made of very thick reinforced concrete were known to be a feature of the Ypres battle; their disposition in great depth without any regard to trench systems, and their indestructibility by modern artillery, had brought a new feature into the war. No absolutely certain way of capturing these 'pill boxes' was ever found; the best way was for the infantry to keep as close to the creeping barrage as they possibly could, and if any 'pill box' still held out the personal initiative of the nearest commander on the spot - using all possible weapons at hand - had to solve the problem.

The 17th Division was transferred to the XIV Corps who were known to be fighting in the Fifth Army north-east of Ypres. The battalion entrained at Saulty at 2 p.m. on October 4th, and after a six hours' journey arrived at Peselhoek - north of Poperinghe - whence they marched to a camp near to St. Sixte (Corps Headquarters). Five days were spent in this vicinity; the difference between the gently rolling Arras country with its chalk substratum and this flat ugly country which held water like a sponge, was very marked. The people too on the border of Belgium and France seemed to possess no nationality or patriotic ideas; they merely looked on empty-eyed at the coming and going of the thousands of troops, apparently not caring to which country they belonged.

The 17th Division took over a portion of the front line on the night October 10/11th. This front lay astride the Ypres - Staden railway which ran absolutely north-eastwards for about 1000 yards into the enemy area. The country is difficult to describe, both because the ground lacked tactical features, and the English language lacks words to express adequately the utter desolation, mud, and misery of the place. Some two miles west of the front line lay the Pilckem Ridge, a gentle rise which had been captured on July 31st. About two miles east of the line was the Stadenberg Ridge which ran southwards to Westroosebeeke and Passchendale. Between these two ridges was a flat desert. A few pavé roads and groups of 'pill boxes' were the only features which had survived the battle. The village of Langemarck was to be seen - distinguished by a huge white mound which had been the village church. The 17th Division relieved the 29th Division who had fought their way forward from the eastern outskirts of Langemarck to about 200 yards beyond a straight well marked pavé road running roughly at right angles to the Ypres - Staden Railway; this road ran parallel to the front line of posts.

A further advance was ordered, and the 51st Brigade were chosen for the attacking troops. On October 9th the 10th Sherwood Foresters relieved troops of the 29th Division in the support area on the eastern outskirts of Langemarck. They occupied the remains of the last enemy trench system in that area; eastwards of that there were no definite lines of trenches, only the concrete pill boxes and small isolated posts made by joining up and enlarging shell holes. The battalion was very unfortunate in losing Capt. J. A.Meads, M.C., at this time; practically a direct hit from a shell killed this officer while moving into the line. He was a very valuable Company Commander, and had been with the battalion since the early days in 1914. He came over to France with it, and had been wounded at the Bluff in February 1916. On the night October 10/11th the battalion moved into the front line, again relieving troops of the 29th Division. The portion of the line held was about 300 yards south of the Ypres - Staden Railway.

On October 11th detailed orders were received for the attack; the Brigade was to advance on a three-battalion frontage behind a very dense creeping barrage. The 10th Sherwood Foresters were the right battalion with troops of the 4th Division on their right flank. To ensure correct direction being obtained at the start of the attack our advanced posts were to withdraw 200 yards to the pavé road. The barrage was to come down immediately east of this road, and an advance of 1200 yards was to be made. 'B' company was the right leading company followed by 'A'; ' D' was the left followed by 'C'.

Zero hour was 5.25 a.m. On October 12th the barrage was very thick and accurate, and the attack was a complete success. On arrival at the first objective (some 600 yards advance) the supporting companies advanced through the leading companies to the final objective. Various groups of 'pill boxes' were captured, the garrisons of which were able to offer little resistance as the troops followed so close behind the barrage. In all, 9 officers and 250 other ranks were captured. Three counter-attacks were attempted by the enemy that day but were all broken up by machine gun fire before reaching our line. The day was fine, but at that time of year the mud never seemed to dry, and moving over the ground was an immensely difficult task. All ranks by the end of the day were smothered from head to foot in mud. But in spite of all, everyone showed themselves determined to stick to the ground they had won and continued to smile. Lieut.-Col. H. J. King received the D.S.O., and Capt. J. N. Knight the M.C. for this action; the way in which the latter despatched a German by shooting a Very Light at him at close quarters tickled everyone's fancy immensely! Casualties were comparatively light; 2nd Lieut. Dorrington was killed, Capt. Cohen and 2nd Lieuts. Ebery, Hanson, and Marchant wounded; there were 165 casualties to other ranks.

On the night 13/14th the battalion was relieved by troops of the 50th Brigade and marched to a camp at Elverdinghe. While on their way out they got the first whiffs of mustard gas which they got to know so well, to their cost, in 1918. The camp was seven miles away; this was a very long march for the men after being in such unspeakable conditions for five days. In large offensive operations in bad weather this seems to be an inevitable evil; the camps are built in the summer and the troops then fight their way further and further forward from them. These huts, however, were exceptionally comfortable.

On October 14th a couple of Gotha bombing planes carried out a daylight raid on Elverdinghe, and repeated their visit the same night. No casualties were caused to the battalion. It was only at this time that the enemy really developed his bombing tactics; the battalion had never experienced anything on a large scale in bombing before, but for the whole of the rest of the winter these raids were frequent.

The battalion moved back to a camp in the vicinity of Proven on the 26th where they rested, reorganized and trained. From here they travelled by buses on the 21st to Sanghen - a small village south of the St. Omer - Calais road, about ten kilometres east of Calais. The whole division moved back to this area and proceeded to settle down for a period of about three weeks. Training was started here on October 22nd; the country was very pleasant; rolling hills and woods, out of the sound of guns, and away from the sight of mud. But on October 24th the bombshell burst; nothing less can be used to describe the news. The 51st Brigade were to go back to the line while the remainder of the Division continued to stay in the rest area!

A certain division holding the line north of the Ypres - Staden Railway had declared its incapability of holding the line under the present conditions without support from some troops other than its own! The 51st Brigade were chosen for this rôle. It was a battalion that found it very difficult to keep cheerful which entrained at Audruicq. They detrained at Proven, remained in a camp close by for a day, and thence went on the 26th by train to Boesinghe. It was impossible to make a start from here for the support area till 7 p.m. owing to the non-arrival of rations. However, by 11.30 p.m. the battalion had relieved troops in the neighbourhood of Widjendrift where they remained for three days. The place needs no description; one place was very much the same as any other in that area -

mud, a few tree stumps, a 'pill box' or two, then more mud.

The battalion was used while here for assisting the R.E., and for a certain amount of carrying to the front line. On the 29th Capt. R.C. Wilmot, Lieut. C. E. S. Cox, M.C., and C.S.M. Allen, were killed; a shell came right into the 'pill box' where they were and killed them all. There were some officers who joined the battalion who never seemed to become part of it in any sense; they were reinforcements - and reinforcements they remained to the end of their days. But there were others who by some subtle means became sooner or later a living part of the battalion, and in thinking of the battalion one always included them as a matter of course. Both Wilmot and Cox belonged to this latter type; whether in the line or in the company mess out in rest, one could not help but realize that they were important to the battalion as good soldiers and good fellows.

On the night October 29/30th the battalion was relieved, and marched back to Boesinghe - thence by train to Proven to the same camp that they occupied on October 25th The 51st Brigade moved to Zermezeele on November 1st (this lay about ten miles west of Proven) for seven days' rest and training. Only a few days were left of the rest which the remainder of the division had been taking, so it was not thought worth while to make the long journey to Sanghen again. The new area was not nearly so good a one as Sanghen; it was too near Belgium, and the whole country suggested that from which the battalion had recently come. Special attention was paid to gas discipline during the rest. The deadly effect of the mustard gas had already been felt by the British Army, and all ranks were warned against it. The 17th Division was now transferred to the XIX Corps, and were therefore holding the same part of the line that the latter formation held in October. The Division which had relieved the 17th Division astride the Ypres-Staden Railway on October 21st had attempted a further advance, but this was unsuccessful, largely owing to the enormous physical effort required to move across the battlefield even without being faced by any opposition. After this failure, no further advances were ordered on this front; it proved sufficiently difficult and costly merely to hold the ground won.

On November 7th Lieut.-Col. King went to England for 10 weeks on the sick list, and Major Daniel took command. On November 9th six officers arrived, including Capt. C. H. Page for the 10th K.O.Y.L.I. who took over duties of adjutant, and Lieut. G. F. March, M.C., from the 2nd Sherwood Foresters who proved such a great mainstay to the battalion from that time until its disbandment.

On November 8th the battalion marched to a camp near Proven where they remained till the 12th; the country round about was so water-logged with heavy rains that route marching was the only form of training that could be done. A move was made to a camp near Elverdinghe on the 13th From here large working parties were sent up to the crest of the Pilckem Ridge to repair some old trench systems, and to erect accommodation in them. Great care had to be taken by these parties to avoid being spotted by the enemy. The weight of the enemy artillery was extraordinarily heavy on this front during October and November; there seemed to be little fire from field guns, but the Hun made up deficiencies in this respect by means of his 15 cm. howitzer (5.9). Any movement seemed to draw a dozen or so of these horrible shells, and in all enemy bombardments the 5.9 seemed to predominate.

On the night 19/20th the battalion relieved troops of the 50th Brigade in the front line; the portion of front held by the division during this tour was practically the same as that which they captured on October 12th, i.e. astride the Ypres - Staden Railway. Relief in this sector was a lengthy process; the battalion marched out of Elverdinghe at 9.15 a.m. on November 19th; a halt was made at Huddlestone camp on the east side of the Ypres - Dixmude canal which was crossed at Boesinghe. Their three days' rations were distributed to the men, and officers gave final instructions to the company quartermaster sergeants not to let them starve while in the line. A few high velocity shells arrived while the battalion was in this camp, causing a dozen casualties. About 3.30 p.m. the battalion marched out of the camp on to the duckboard tracks going towards the line; the roads east of the canal were generally too congested with traffic or else too deep in mud to make it worthwhile to walk on them. The men had to go in single file with intervals between platoons, so that the battalion spread out over a great distance. The Pilckem Ridge could not be crossed till dusk, but in this case the enemy either saw the first party of troops who crossed the ridge or else he expected a relief, for he put down a stiff barrage of his favourite 5.9s on to the duckboard track from the top of the ridge to the Steenbeek - a swampy stream which lay at its foot. There was nothing for it but to run the gauntlet, and we got off lightly with only four killed and fourteen wounded. East of the Steenbeek things became quieter again, and it was just a slow trudge along the single track past Langemarck and up to the pavé road which was the starting line on October 12th There the companies branched off in charge of their guides to their respective positions, often following a tape which had been laid across the trackless swamp. It was midnight before all companies had reported 'Relief complete'.

After three days in the line the battalion was relieved by the 7th Border

Regt. and withdrew to the support area, half the battalion east of Langemarck and the other half on the Pilckem Ridge. On the 25th the battalion was relieved by troops of the 52nd Brigade and withdrew to a camp at Elverdinghe.

The actual physical effort required to live in the forward area was so great that divisions could only remain a short time in the line without a rest. By the time an average man (and many men of the recent drafts were below the average physically) had spent five or six days in muddy little trenches and shell holes in the front line and support area, and had marched back all the weary miles to Elverdinghe, he was more than ordinarily tired, in some cases exhausted; and although it might not show on the surface, he was not as fit as he was at first by the time he had to go back into the line. Complete rests away from the line had to be frequent.

The 17th Division was relieved on December 3rd. The battalion was still at Elverdinghe and marched back to Proven, and thence on the 9th they again took train for Sanghen. A letter from the Division stated that three or four weeks' rest might be expected, then presumably we were for the Langemarck - Pilckem area once again. But another bombshell arrived - The end of November and the first week of December had seen the capture of Bourlon Wood, the German counter-attack, and finally the withdrawal of the British line from the wood. Divisions on that front were tired and fought out; the 17th Division were selected to act as relieving troops; they were transferred to the V Corps fighting on that front, and transferred quickly to Bapaume.

I doubt if any troops ever left the line at Ypres reluctantly or with any regrets; the 10th Sherwood Foresters were no exception to this, and they turned their backs on Belgium for the second and last time, heartily thankful to get away. Everyone felt that whatever the south had in store for them it could not be quite so monotonously hideous as the battlefield which they had just left.

CHAPTER V

Cambrai and the March Push

The battalion moved to Nordausques on the St. Omer - Calais road on December 12th and were at one hour's notice to move. On the 14th they entrained at Wizerne, and after twelve hours in the train reached Bapaume. From here they marched to huts at Barastre. The weather had turned cold and the ground was hard with frost. Five days were spent here and a certain amount of training was done. It was rather extraordinary to be so near the scene of our labours and flounderings of a year ago, though under such different circumstances. A few people went over the area west of Le Transloy to see if they could recognize the old line; they found the dugouts still intact where Battalion H.Q. had been, but Eclipse - Zenith - Misty and Gusty Trenches and the rest could hardly be recognized, so much were they fallen in and overgrown by a year's crop of weeds.

The 17th Division took over a portion of the front line extending from Flesquieres inclusive (right boundary) to a few hundred yards east of the Canal du Nord, and relieved the 59th Division.

The main feature of the country is first and foremost Bourlon Wood which rose in a great mound about a mile behind the enemy's front line; it is a very commanding position and we all quickly found that again and again when in a fold in the ground we were completely out of sight of the enemy except for the trees on the top of Bourlon Wood. In the British area there was a well-marked ridge running east and west, on which stands

Hermies, Havrincourt and Flesquieres. The Canal du Nord runs north and south and cuts through this ridge at a point midway between Hermies and Havrincourt in a cutting about 200 feet deep. The canal to the north of Havrincourt has smooth brick sides. The Hindenburg line ran south of Havrincourt, thence north-westwards, crossing the Canal du Nord, thence northwards to Moevres. The Hindenburg support line ran south of Flesquieres thence north-westwards for about 2000 yards, thence it turned north and ran parallel to the canal on its east bank.

The line to which the British troops had withdrawn was so arranged that the forward posts were in advance of the portion of the Hindenburg line, which was mentioned above as running north-west, while the main line of resistance would be the Hindenburg support line itself. At the point where this line turned north, the British line turned west - cutting the Canal du Nord and the Hindenburg line at right angles, and rejoining our original front line before the November advance close to Demicourt. (This all sounds like Euclid, but it should be clear with the aid of a map. W.N.H.)

On December 20th the battalion moved up to the old British front line (O.B.L.) in Havrincourt Wood at Butler's Cross, and relieved the 2/8th Sherwood Foresters, and on the following night they relieved the troops of the London Regiment in a sector of the front line between Flesquieres and the Canal du Nord.

The weather continued cold and frosty with a little snow on the ground. The battalion sector faced Graincourt which was just behind the enemy front line. Signs of the British advance were seen both in our own and in the enemy's forward area; 18 pounder positions and derelict tanks everywhere, a hurriedly laid Decauville railway ran into No Man's Land, old transport lines were seen just behind our front trenches. The most welcome find was a huge dump of petrol and oil for the use of tanks, which was located a few hundred yards inside our lines; the great majority of this was salvaged, but an occasional tin or two was found very useful for the Primus Stove in the R.A.P., and also for persuading the company mess brazier to burn when it was sulky. Captain Marsh was successful in burning his dugout down with some of the petrol.

The Hindenburg support line was a wonderfully fortified position. It had obviously been captured solely with the aid of tanks, for the trenches were almost undamaged by artillery, and the broad tank tracks could be seen running through the belts of wire which were usually about ten yards wide. The enemy artillery remained quiet, a blessed change from the line near Langemarck, and most of the firing seemed to be done with 77 mm guns - the German field guns. A certain subaltern was heard to remark, while being shelled by these whizz-bangs, that he really did not mind as long as they kept those d****d 5.9's quiet!

But the best part of the whole sector seemed to be that there was firm turf and good roads to walk on instead of a desert churned up by innumerable shell holes so thick that they touched one another. It was fortunate that the enemy's attitude was quiet for our forward line of posts were very shallow indeed, with little or no wire in front, and could not be approached by day without coming under close enemy observation. Work was at once begun on deepening the front trenches, linking up the gaps between the posts, and digging communication trenches. The enemy, on the other hand, in this area again showed very little activity as regards digging, and in the first months of 1918 this difference became more and more marked. Nowhere did he seem to dig with real energy, especially in the very forward area, while our lines of defence continued to be dug deep and well, and were well wired. On the evening of Christmas Day the battalion was relieved by the 7th Border Regiment and withdrew to a support position; two companies and Battalion Headquarters were in cellars in Havrincourt village, and two companies in the Hindenburg line just outside the village. Ample accommodation for these was found in the enormous number of deep dugouts which were situated in this line. The battalion remained in this position until the night of 30th/31st when the 51st Brigade was relieved by the 52nd Brigade, and they then moved to the O.B.L. in Havrincourt Wood.

Almost from the time of arrival in the Third Army, the Higher Command had talked of the probability of an enemy offensive on a very large scale which would include this portion of the line east of Havrincourt Wood; these warnings, vague at first, became more and more definite as the first months of 1918 wore on. There was little enough to see superficially by a glance at the enemy line or by observing his artillery activity; up to the outbreak of his great offensive he never dug systems which could possibly have been used as assembly trenches, and his artillery never became very active, nor did he do any wire cutting. On our side every preparation was made to meet the expected storm. Officers and men always groused at the policy of 'Defend, Defend' instead of 'Prepare to advance', and they said it was bad for morale, but the preparations were fortunately very thorough indeed. When the enemy, early in January, showed no sign of further offensive intentions in the near future, the 17th Division extended their front to the left taking in the Canal du Nord, the divisional boundary was about 600 yards west of this. The Fifth Corps' front was then held by three divisions, with the 17th Division on the left. The Corps' front was in a large salient, the tip of which was on the front of the centre division at

Ribecourt. Strong lines of defence were dug behind the front line; the general idea was that they should join the two sides of the salient by a straight line to serve as defensive positions should the nose of the salient be driven in. Early in March, lines still farther behind the line were begun in order to co-ordinate the defensive lines throughout the Third Army front. It is important to note that the main energies of the Corps were directed in order to meet a frontal attack on the salient which they held.

To return to the narrative, the 51st Brigade in a support area in Havrincourt Wood relieved troops of the 2nd Division holding the front line astride the Canal du Nord on the night January 3rd/4th This relief was the extension of front held by 7the 17th Division mentioned above and was a complicated one; the 10th Sherwood Foresters relieved portions of three separate battalions. To make matters still more complicated the enemy made a small attack at dusk on the front which the battalion was going to take over. About half a dozen isolated posts had been dug some hundred yards in front of the actual front line trench; they were poorly defended as regards wire, and the enemy by means of a sudden attack simultaneously captured all these posts. When the Sherwood Foresters arrived in the front line they found that one or two counter-attacks had already been made, but without success. The troops holding the line naturally did not want to leave it before doing their utmost to recapture the posts, and they remained in order to make further attacks. These, however, were unsuccessful, the enemy was thoroughly on the alert, and finally the 2nd Division were obliged to give up the attempt. Relief was complete at 2 a.m. These posts were never recaptured, and the enemy subsequently linked them up by a trench to his own front line.

The battalion remained in this part of the line till January 9th. The enemy activity was very slight.

The sector held was on the east bank of the canal, and on the west bank just behind the enemy front line was a great heap of spoil 30 feet high made from the earth and chalk dug from the canal. This slag heap* held many trench mortars which were a continual annoyance to our troops within their range. Artillery fire had little effect on them as they were dug in so deeply, though our own 6 inch Newton mortars were usually able to silence them.

The frost and snow continued, making trench life quite bearable. On January 9th the 7th Border Regiment relieved the battalion which withdrew to cellars and dugouts in Hermies. While living here they worked on the defences which were being dug on the northern and eastern outskirts of the village. Tunnelling companies were at work making deep dugouts, and these required shifts of men working eight hours each shift to help remove the soil; the remainder of the battalion worked mainly on trench digging. A thaw set in on the 10th, but cellars were on the whole watertight, and roads were good, so that the change in weather did not affect the garrison of the village very much.

A further tour of duty in the line was ordered, and on the night 16/17th the battalion relieved the 7th Border Regiment in the same sector as before. The thaw had been followed by rain, and the trenches, particularly the communication trenches, were in a fearful state of mud; it was practically impossible to go along the top of the trench as a large number of belts of barbed wire would have proved serious obstacles.

(After the Armistice I examined this slag heap and found it honeycombed with very deep dugouts and well dug emplacements which could only have been destroyed by delay-action shells of a very heavy calibre.)

The men were wearing thigh gumboots, the mud had reached a consistency between putty and treacle in the worst parts. Many of the men stuck fast in this quagmire; some were dug out in their long boots, others could only be pulled out leaving the boots behind in the mud; these unhappy wretches had to walk back to Hermies in their stockinged feet! The boots left in the mud were never completely recovered; they were cut to pieces by the party who dug out the trenches later. A long correspondence started between the battalion and some extraordinary Staff Officer miles away in the rear; he endeavoured to make the battalion pay for the boots lost! Long after the Hun offensive had taken place when the battalion were many leagues away from Hermies, this correspondence was dragging out its weary length I never heard what became of it, how it ended, or indeed, whether it is ended yet, but those of us who knew Lieut. - Col. King can be sure that the Staff Officer must have been particularly clever if the boots were ever paid for.

The front line when it was finally reached was found to be less muddy; the tumbling in of the trenches had been kept within bounds by the Border Regiment.

Only two days were spent in the line, after which time the battalion was relieved by troops of the 52nd Brigade and went back to a hutted camp between Hertincourt and Haplincourt, part of the way by light railway. This was the first time since December 20th that the men had been in any sort of camp where they could get a bath and a change of clothes. Everyone very much enjoyed getting clean again and returning to the best sort of civilization which could be obtained in that part of the country. The amusements mainly consisted of the 'pictures' in Bertincourt and the Officers' Club, a heaven-sent institution where there were no closed hours for drinks. But it was Eden without Eve, for these villages had been completely wrecked by the enemy who had retired from them in March 1917, and the civilians had been driven eastwards by the retiring Hun; the nearest Francaise in a westward direction was Albert, about twenty miles away. A regular programme of Brigade and battalion reliefs was worked out for the divisional front, the same system was adhered to as was adopted at Arras; two Brigades held the divisional front, each Brigade after doing twelve days in the line was relieved by the third Brigade which had been resting. About this time the composition of each Brigade was cut down to the three battalion basis, so that the resting brigade had two battalions in hutted camps on the Bertincourt - Haplincourt road, and the third battalion in cellars in Hermies. Of the Brigades holding the line, only one battalion was in the front line, the other two were disposed in great depth in positions of support and reserve. A period of regular trench warfare started which was only terminated by the outbreak of the German offensive on March 21st.

On February 9th the 8th South Staffordshire Regiment was disbanded, this being the battalion of the 51st Brigade which was selected to serve as reinforcements to other battalions of the same regiment. Our relations with this unfortunate battalion had always been very good; its fine fighting qualities were unquestionable, and it was with genuine regret that we saw them depart. Major W. Gibson, M.C. of the 8th South Staffordshire Regiment was transferred temporarily to the 10th Sherwood Foresters.

On January 1st Major T. W. Daniel, D.S.O., M.C. proceeded to Aldershot for a ten weeks' course at the Senior Officers' School. Major C. H. Page assumed duties of Second in Command, and Captain S. S. Moseley became Acting Adjutant.

About this time Lieut. T. P. C. Wilson returned to the battalion. He had been appointed Staff - Captain of the 51st Brigade early in 1917, but he was now 'ungummed' and returned to regimental duty. There was much to be said on both sides as to his fitness for a staff appointment, and stirring up old mud is not the intention of this history; but he made a fine regimental officer during the short time he was with the battalion, until he was killed on March 21st. He threw every part of his keenness and energy into the work, and was promoted Captain in February. The man himself was extraordinarily interesting; he contributed several truly witty articles to 'Punch' - notably 'David' in 1917, and had published verse in several papers; altogether he was a gay light-hearted modern of the best type.

Fairly quiet tours in the line followed one another. The enemy from the beginning of February was very chary about occupying his forward posts.

It will be remembered that at this time many raids to secure identification took place on the British front, but in a large number of cases the raiding parties found that the enemy had evacuated his front line. This behaviour was probably ordered, so as to avoid the capture of even a single prisoner from whom the Hun intentions might be learnt. On February 23rd a strong patrol of the 10th Sherwood Foresters attempted to obtain identification on the east bank of the canal, but the advanced posts of the enemy were found empty, while his main line was strongly wired and evidently held by a large garrison. The party had to return unsuccessful.

The defensive works on the divisional front were continually worked on, and by the beginning of March were nearing completion. This particularly applied to a strong line dug on the northern slopes of the Hermies - Havrincourt ridge. The action of the divisional troops in the event of an attack was carefully worked out, down to the last platoon, and in early March all infantry of the division practised the actual movements which took place on the morning of March 21st, including the manning of the Hermies - Havrincourt line.

Some weeks before the outbreak of the offensive the enemy fired a certain amount of mustard gas on our front; Havrincourt was his favourite target. It was realized later that the firing of this special type of gas on any point meant that the enemy did not intend to make a direct frontal attack on that part, but rather to capture it by outflanking it. From March 7th onwards the offensive was expected daily; special artillery programmes were carried out, generally in the early hours of the morning, along the whole of the Third Army front several times during March. The 19th and 20th were calm and still; a heavy haze prevented any observation of the enemy except his front line. This haze must have helped him enormously in the final concentration of troops and artillery.

The 10th Sherwood Foresters were in huts in Bertincourt on the 20th, having been relieved in the line on the 17th. The night was quiet, and a subaltern at Divisional H.Q. was sleepily signing a wire to Corps H.Q. 'Situation quiet - nothing to report' when the thing started. There was no mistake about this being 'Der Tag'. The air suddenly seemed to be alive with high velocity shells, a shower of these arrived periodically in Bertincourt, and high up could be heard the hurried shuffling noise of enormous fellows going over to Rocquigny, Bapaume and elsewhere.

The battalion 'stood to' as a matter of course, and quickly received orders from Brigade to move to battle positions. This was some 1000 yards outside the village in the vicinity of a large slag heap on the Bertincourt - Hermies road. The shelling made the exit from the village unhealthy, but as there were few casualties during this move the battalion was soon ready to go on to any part of the divisional front which required reinforcement. About midday it became clear the only very minor attacks were being made on the divisional front, and the division on the right also reported its line intact. On the left, however, the 51st Division had been heavily attacked and their left flank had been driven in some considerable distance, so that the portion of their front which still held firm was now threatened from the left rear. In consequence, two companies of the 10th Sherwood Foresters, under Major Gibson, about noon were ordered to man the defences of the left of Hermies, which village was being held by the 7th Lincolnshire Regiment. The remainder of the battalion at 3 p.m. were sent to the same position, as the situation on the left flank became still more acute. The defences of Hermies formed roughly a right angle with the village lying at the point of the angle. On the right the trench joined the Havrincourt defences, on the left the line called Jargon Trench bent backwards - running approximately along the divisional boundary towards Velu Wood. By 5 p.m. the whole battalion was in position; two companies in Jargon Trench and two in the bank of the Velu - Hermies railway which served as a support line to the trench. South of the V Corps front the enemy had penetrated our lines deeply, so that as soon as night fell it was decided to withdraw from the entire forward area on the Corps front; the 17th Division in consequence withdrew to the Havrincourt - Hermies line. The 51st Division on the left attempted to prolong this line northwards, but this defensive system in their area was only poorly dug and in some cases only imaginary. In the early hours of March 22nd the enemy followed up our withdrawal and forced the 51st Division to their next position some 2,500 yards in rear. This left a huge gap between the left of the 17th Division at Hermies and the right of the 51st Division. The 10th Sherwood Foresters and the 7th Border Regiment on their left did their utmost to fill this gap, six guns of the Motor Machine Gun Corps also lent invaluable aid.

Jargon Trench had only been very recently dug, and the enemy artillery was evidently unaware of its existence for few shells fell in and round it. The village of Hermies seemed to interest the Hun gunners particularly, and this target absorbed most of the shell fire while only a few shells fell on the defenders who were all outside.

All the morning the enemy were seen massing in and around Doignies, several attacks were made on Jargon Trench, but they were all broken up by artillery and machine gun fire with very heavy enemy casualties. The gap on the left became larger and larger, and the enemy - as soon as he realized its existence - poured all his troops into it. At 12.45 p.m. he had captured

Velu Wood which completely turned the whole of the 17th Divisional front; orders from the Division for a withdrawal from the Hermies defences had gone out at 11 a.m.; these reached the front line troops at 1 p.m. The withdrawal was carried out in good order; before the last men of the Sherwood Foresters had left Jargon Trench the enemy had completely worked round their left flank and many of our fellows were killed by machine guns as they tried to cross the bank of the Hermies - Velu Railway. Lieut. R. A. Page with a small party tried to get across from a point nearer Hermies, but was unfortunately captured.

The battalion was ordered to withdraw through the 63rd Division who were holding a line on the eastern outskirts of Bertincourt, and to concentrate west of Villers-au-Flos. Before the line held by the 63rd Division was reached we suffered more casualties from the enemy who had now worked forward from Velu Wood with machine guns. Captain T. P. C. Wilson was killed in this way. Major C. H. Page with two companies held a line of defence between Hermies and Bertincourt until the remainder of the 51st Brigade had passed through; he then followed them.

The withdrawal was unquestionably a fine manoeuvre; the enemy had suffered severely in his attacks in the morning while all our men were able to break off the engagement exactly at the right minute and to get away with few casualties. It was a dry, dusty march to Villers-au-Flos, and the men already showed signs of fatigue after their sleepless night and a strenuous morning. By midnight the battalion was concentrated in huts near the village which a little time before had held men attached to Corps Headquarters.

The line held by the 63rd Division east of Bertincourt was prolonged in a southerly direction and ran east of Ytres; it was in a good state of defence and expected to hold for some little time. It caused no small consternation when the enemy broke through this line very early on the 23rd at Ytres. This was the last defensive position on the Corps front which had been worked on at all recently. Westwards lay the Somme battlefield with its old lines of trenches and tangles of rusty wire in much the same state in which they had been left in the spring of 1917; there was no solid position like the Hermies - Havrincourt line to fall back on. The 52nd Brigade were pushed out to hold the enemy by Bus (west of Ytres), and the 51st Brigade supported them in an old enemy defensive position running east of Rocquigny and southwards to Sailly-Saillisel; the Sherwood Foresters were on the left holding Rocquigny. About noon the enemy had worked round the northern flank of the position, and the battalion was obliged to fall back: they stood again west of Rocquigny until the other two battalions of the Brigade had withdrawn, and they were then ordered to withdraw still further and concentrate at Martinpuich. In this engagement the enemy used his machine guns with great effect, taking every advantage of cover they wound their way forward with an almost uncanny quickness, and were able to outflank one position after another.

The march to Martinpuich was a weary trudge; all the roads were merely narrow overgrown tracks, and it was impossible to keep the men together in any definite formation. Neither officers nor men knew what was happening to the north or south of them, or why there was all this sickening withdrawing, and it was impossible to avoid the attitude: 'I don't know or care what happens, but let's stop this marching westwards.'

The last parties of the battalion arrived at Martinpuich at midnight; some huts were found which had belonged to an obscure Labour Corps unit. Some of the men were too tired to eat and some too hungry to go to sleep, but at any rate it was a rest from the eternal overgrown shell holes, over which they had come that afternoon. No orders had been received about further moves, and there was, as far as we knew, no definite line of troops between us and advancing enemy. During the day units had become very much scattered, divisions did not know exactly where their Brigades were, battalions seemed to push off into the blue, only turning up long afterwards, and all this added to the uneasiness about what was going to happen next. As a matter of fact, the effect of the enormous retreat of the Fifth Army was being felt in the Third Army front; away to the south the enemy was across the Somme and still advancing.

The V Corps were ordered to take up a line Montauban - Bazentin le Petit - Martinpuich with the 17th Division holding from Montauban to Bazentin le Grand. It was entirely owing to the efforts of the Brigade Major - Captain E. Walker of the Bays - of the 51st Brigade that these orders reached the troops of the Brigade.

At 4am. on March 24th the battalion moved across country to Montauban; the knowledge of the country by the old stagers who had seen the Somme battle was invaluable at this point. Maps were few and of very small scale, but anyone who went through the Somme battle knew Montauban with Cosy Corner close by. When we arrived, no trace of any other troops could be seen; there was no artillery fire; nothing except the worn out appearance of the men suggested that we were out for a real battle, and not just a Brigade field day. The orders from Divisional Headquarters never reached the other Brigades who only put in an appearance much later in the day, and it was quickly seen that the 51st Brigade would have to hold the entire Divisional front. This was done, with the Sherwood foresters on the right holding east of north of Montauban. Some rather disorganized troops of the 9th Division were discovered near Bernafay Wood on the right, also troops of a cavalry brigade; they knew as little as we did about the general situation. There was still no sign of the enemy; it seemed as though the weather was going to be the same as on the previous days, warm with a slight mist, which made artillery observation difficult. About 10 a.m. small bodies of the enemy were seen moving in Longueval and High Wood; they did not seem to be massing on our front for an attack. At about this time our own artillery started to shell the line held by the battalion; it seemed to be the last straw on top of days of enormous strain and fatigue. Who the gunners were, or who they thought we were, was never found out, but the line had to be drawn in some hundreds of yards.

About noon heavy enemy attacks developed north and south of the Divisional front; the enemy captured Maricourt away to the south, and Montauban was in danger of being outflanked. A further withdrawal was ordered to a line running north and south through Fricourt. The 52nd Brigade had by this time come up and held the northern half of the Divisional front. It was annoying to retire to this new position with hardly a shot fired, for although large bodies of the enemy had been seen in the distance they had never attempted a regular attack on our front. The new line was taken at about 5pm., but there was still no sign of the enemy on our front.

At dusk it was decided that other divisions should hold the line Albert - Meaulte - Bray, and that the 17th Division should withdraw through this line at night, and should then be used where most needed. This movement was carried out without any interference from the enemy who never gained touch with our troops. The road through Meaulte which some of us knew so well was good, and the night was fine with a moon; things seemed a little brighter, and some cheery soldier started a song. We were ordered to concentrate at Henencourt, west of Albert.

Along the roads was seen the most pitiful of all sights - refugees from Meaulte and Dernancourt. The flight of the civilians has been so often described and drawn, but the actual thing defies description. One does not mind so much the fighting, the marching, the sleeplessness, but to see these poor scared creatures with all their worldly goods in a perambulator, with a kiddie stumbling alongside, seems to be essentially wrong and utterly abhorrent.

The morning of March 25th was spent in Henencourt; the cookers were there, and the men got a good feed and a little sleep. The whole division was crammed into one village, and the main streets looked like nothing so much as 'Goose Fair' but without the girls and the roundabouts.

About noon the news arrived that the enemy had broken through at Hebuterne with armoured cars; the division moved at once to Senlis before it was found that the news was untrue and a further move was cancelled. As a matter of fact, some over zealous officer - we heard - had mistaken one of our own whippet tanks (then a new weapon) for Boche engines of frightfulness ! But this was followed quickly by serious news; the enemy had broken the Albert - Bray line and was in Dernancourt, south-west of Albert. The 52nd Brigade pushed off in a south-easterly direction to hold the high ground north of Dernancourt; the 51st Brigade moved in support to Millencourt. The battalion arrived in that village about 9 p.m. and spent the night in empty houses. In the morning there was a refreshing change for there was no sudden move to fight an unlocated enemy; our troops seemed to be holding him at Dernancourt and west of Albert. Millencourt had been left hurriedly by the inhabitants and many good things were found. Various sheep and a calf or two were adopted by the lucky ones who came across them, but the French authorities did not appreciate this display of affection and confiscated most of these later. Poultry was plentiful, and all men had a good meal.

Australian troops passed through the village about 11 a.m. moving towards Dernancourt. Soon after, the enemy artillery caught up his infantry and commenced shelling the village; the battalion was ordered to evacuate it and dig in on the western outskirts. Two days were spent in these positions; the posts were dug irregularly, distributed in depth so that a counter-attack could be launched towards Albert when needed.

To all intents and purposes this was the end of the great German offensive so far as the 10th Sherwood Foresters were concerned; only comparatively minor operations took place on this front, and the enemy got no further than Dernancourt and the western bank of the Ancre up to Beaucourt.

Compared with the overwhelming attacks experienced by troops at other parts of the British front, the enemy actions against the battalion were slight. Casualties were correspondingly light, those for the whole month of March being:-

	Killed	Wounded	Missing
Officers	2	5	1
O.R.	24	120	52

The entire weight of the enemy forces never seemed to be directed full on to the battalion front, and the constant withdrawals owing to the left or right flank being turned gave an unsatisfactory feeling to the whole business.

Major C. H. Page was awarded the D.S.O., and Lieut. L. Jacques the Military Cross for gallant conduct during these operations.

On the evening of March 27th the battalion was suddenly ordered to relieve troops of the 35th Brigade (12th Division) in the line immediately west of Albert. When the area was reached which was occupied by the battalion of the 35th Brigade, the position of the forward posts was found to be extremely uncertain. The garrisons had apparently withdrawn before relief arrived. The Sherwood Foresters, however, took up positions as far forward as they could go, and dug in in the dark with entrenching tools. The next day was quiet on our front. On the right the enemy made several attacks on the Australians but was heavily repulsed. On the 29th the battalion was relieved by troops of the 52nd Brigade, and on relief went into billets at Henencourt, forming part of the reserve Brigade of the Division.

The Division was relieved in the line on April 2nd by the 12th Division. The 10th Sherwood Foresters marched to Warloy and thence by easy stages during the next five days to Domart - a village ten miles west of the Doullen -Amiens road. Reinforcements arrived here in great numbers; they were a small part of the fabulous quantities of men which were mentioned in the papers as pouring over to France. 216 O.R. of the Royal Welsh Fusiliers arrived, and they caused much consternation by insisting on writing passionate letters in Welsh to their ladyloves; one unfortunate officer in a moment of weakness confessed that he could read the language, so daily he had a young mountain of letters to censor. Another draft of 231 O.R. arrived; these consisted mainly of 19 year old conscripts, and from now onwards the large majority of the reinforcements were these boys, most of whom had been only six weeks in khaki. With much more training, most of them could have been turned into efficient soldiers; the opportunity for this could not be given, for after four days the battalion marched eastwards again to Talmas, and on April 12th moved to Acheux - a village about six miles behind our front line.

The enemy had been definitely held in the V. Corps front which extended from Beaumont-Hamel to the northern outskirts of Albert. The original plan had been for our troops to hold all the western bank of the Ancre, the main defence to be on the heights, while advanced posts were to be established close to the river bank.

This had not been carried out altogether, for the enemy had crossed the Ancre and had seized some valuable high ground, known as W,15.a., between Albert and Aveluy Wood. In addition to this he had launched a heavy attack westwards from Aveluy early in April, forcing our line backwards halfway through Aveluy Wood. When the 17th Division arrived to relieve the Naval Division on April 14th, the line taken over ran through the middle of the wood; northwards of that we held about 400 yards of the Albert - Miraumont railway which ran close to the river, thence the line bent back to our old front line of 1916 in front of Beaumont-Hamel. It will be thus seen that the enemy had some more or less slight footing along the whole of the western bank of the river except for the 200 yards north of Aveluy Wood which we held. This position jutted out like a mushroom from our lines and could only be approached by shallow communication trenches which ran down the western slopes of the Ancre; these were very steep and under close enemy observation.

The 10th Sherwood Foresters relieved the 4th Bedfordshire Regiment on this front on the night April 15/16th The front taken over included about 600 yards of Aveluy Wood and also the 200 yards of the railway; the other portion of the railway was held by troops of the 50th Brigade. Major T. W. Daniel was in command, and Major C. H. Page acted as Adjutant.

The enemy artillery was considerably active, especially during the next days on the high ground east of Mesnil. The Hun had perfect observation of our forward defences from the heights round Thiepval, and any movement of our men was quickly engaged.

The trenches were still very shallow and casualties were constantly occurring. On April 21st the enemy became particularly active with 5.9's on the whole of the western slopes of the river north of Aveluy Wood. From 9 a.m. to 6 p.m. there was no news from Captain F. B. Joyce, M.C. who was in command of two platoons of 'C' Company holding the positions on the railway. It was impossible to see that part of the line from any positions in rear owing to the smoke, and also because the very steep convex slope of the hill hid it from view even by day. The C.O. expected an attack, and warned the Brigade headquarters. During the afternoon the shelling increased in intensity; and at 6 p.m. two runners arrived from 'C' Company saying that when they left at 5.15 p.m. the company had already suffered heavy casualties and that Captain Joyce had fired two S.O.S. rockets as the enemy had been seen massing on the northern edge of the Wood, and an attack had begun. These rockets had not been seen at Battalion Headquarters, and patrols from the support positions were pushed down the slopes towards the railway, but the shelling was so heavy that it was not till 1a.m. on the 22nd that absolutely definite news was received that the enemy had captured the whole of our position on the railway and were holding it in strength The C.O. had already been reconnoitring the position with a view to a counter - attack; orders were then received that this attack should take place in conjunction with the 50th Brigade - whose line was also lost - at 4.30 a.m. 'B' Company under Lieut. Jacques performed this operation. They advanced down the slopes under the barrage, but when about 100 yards from the railway a devastating enfilade machine gun fire was opened from the northern edge of Aveluy Wood, which caused very heavy casualties to the attackers. No further headway could be made, and they were obliged to withdraw to their jumping-off positions. A smaller operation on the right flank by two platoons of 'D' Company succeeded in driving the enemy out of a group of huts on the northern edge of Aveluy Wood; the huts were then set on fire.

Casualties in this fight were heavy; none of the garrison of the posts on the railway got back to our lines except the two men mentioned above. Captain Joyce's body was found later in August when the enemy had withdrawn across the Ancre. 'B' Company also suffered 70 casualties, a large proportion of whom were missing - presumed killed; many of their bodies were found on August 23rd during the advance.

A good deal of controversy arose concerning the loss of the posts and the failure of the counter-attack. To one whose sympathies are rather with the man on the spot, and not with the officer in safer quarters whose reputation is in danger, the position seemed to be a crazy one. It was impossible to see the position from anywhere in rear, being at the bottom of a very steep convex hill under close enemy observation, and entirely enfiladed by him from both north and south The railway could only be approached by night when it is impossible to see much or to try to criticise. The garrison of 'C' company evidently stuck it out, and the men were either killed or captured. Anyone who knew Captain Joyce can imagine that he would allow no retirement to take place, and that he himself would be killed sooner than be captured. A more gallant gentleman never lived.

Nothing further was attempted by either side in the way of an offensive operation during the remainder of the tour in the line, and in fact, April 21st was the last time that the Hun proved to be 'top-dog' as far as the battalion was concerned; after that time it was we who were to be the attackers and finally victors.

The 7th Border Regt. relieved the battalion in the line on the night 24/25th, and after relief they took up a position of reserve north-west of Martinsart. Working parties for trench digging and all the other routine work of trench warfare once more became the usual thing. Lines of defence on a large scale were planned, for the enemy were still thought to be contemplating large offensive schemes; captured documents subsequently proved that these had actually been planned out in great detail, but owing to the various internal causes and threats on other portions of the western front, the enemy never launched the attack.

A large defensive system was started running east of Mailly Maillet, east of Englebelmer, thence southwards to Millencourt. The whole system was known as the Purple Line, and the digging and wiring of this absorbed most of the battalion working parties.

Ordinary trench warfare followed until the 17th Division was relieved on May 8th The battalion spent from the 4th to the 8th in the front line immediately north of Mesnil but nothing of note occurred. The enemy activity, especially with artillery, slackened very much indeed, and work on the trenches proceeded apace.

The enemy on this particular front was in a nasty position. Immediately behind his front line stretching some fifteen miles eastwards lay the desert of the Somme battlefield; all the other roads except the main Albert - Bapaume road were in a horrible condition, the slightest rain must have made them almost impassable for transport. In the very foremost area he held a more or less precarious position on the west of the Ancre; our artillery were continually smashing up his bridges across this swampy stream. The only outstanding advantages were that he held the Thiepval ridge which commanded an extensive view of our lines, and also the broken nature of the ground made it very easy for him to hide his artillery; on an aeroplane photograph small tracks and the litter round the gun pits all merged into the mass of shell holes and wreckage which covered the battlefield, while our batteries standing in an open field were impossible to hide from the air. But his infantry had nothing to go back to rest in, except old huts and bivouacs, while behind us lay inhabited villages with woods and open fields.

After relief by troops of the Naval Division on May 8th, the battalion marched to the Bois Creftel, a large wood near Toutencourt. No sooner had they arrived there than they were ordered back to billets in Lealvillers. From here very large working parties were sent to work on a large defensive system near Beaussart, the Brown Line. On May 18th they started a short rest. Beauquesnes was reached after two days march, and all ranks had a rest in good billets in decent weather for five days. The Corps Commander - Lieut.-General Cameron Shute - inspected the battalion here, and congratulated it on its smart turnout.

On the 25th we marched back to Acheux and moved to bivouacs north of Forceville on the 27th, becoming part of the reserve brigade of the 17th Division. The front taken over by the division for this tour was immediately north of the part held at the end of April. It faced Beaumont Hamel on the left, and the front line coincided almost exactly with the line our troops held before the battle of the Somme started; the enormous mine crater blown on July 1st, 1916 was still a very outstanding landmark, and some of the old wire was still in existence. The divisional front as usual was held by two brigades abreast; the third brigade was accommodated in shelters between Beaussart and Forceville. At this date, Lieut. - Col. King returned to England sick, and took over command again from Major Daniel on about July 16th

A period of regular and rather dull trench warfare started which lasted till June 23rd. Very little of importance occurred. On June 11th 2nd Lieut. W. Stevenson was in charge of a patrol in No Man's Land examining a large crater when he met an enemy patrol; this officer and two men were wounded and taken prisoner. The 17th Division was relieved on June 23rd when the battalion marched to a canvas camp near Herissart. They stayed there till July 9th Training and all the usual routine work when out of the line was undertaken. During this rest, a highly successful Horse Show was held at Rubempre, and a Brigade show at Toutencourt, where Charles Reynard's mules had many successes. The assembly of the 17th Division in case of attack was practised on the night July 7/8th; it was supposed to be a dead secret known only to Staff-Officers, but some of these are mercifully human, and when the alarm came about 11.30 p.m. no one was in bed! A long dark march some eight miles across country completed the manoeuvre, and then in the early dawn, with an empty stomach and with tobacco tasting like damp weed, we were told we might go home! Immediately on arrival back to our tents at Herissart, advance parties had to go forward preparatory to a divisional relief in the line. The remainder of the battalion followed early on the morning of July 9th and relieved troops of the 12th Division in the line immediately south of Aveluy Wood. Another period of very quiet trench warfare started. The line needs little description; most of it was very much overlooked by the high ground (W.15.a.) away to the south, but the enemy did not seem to use this point of vantage for 'strafing' purposes.

American officers and men were attached to the battalion for instruction while in this sector; at first individual officers and N.C.O.'s were attached, later complete companies came and spent 48 hours in the line; they usually left reluctantly.

On July 26th one of our patrols was surprised in Aveluy Wood, and two men were missing. The wood was full of very thick tangled undergrowth, and the lines were almost ridiculously close together at one point.

CHAPTER VI

The Return Push
I. With the Australians

Towards the end of July it became more and more apparent that all was not well with the Hun morale generally; immensely heavy artillery shoots were carried out on the enemy area on the west bank of the Ancre to make him still more tired of life. A 15 inch howitzer was told off specially to knock Aveluy causeway to pieces, which was the only main crossing used by the enemy. These measures had the desired effects, for on August 2nd the enemy abandoned all the area that he had held west of the Ancre. The 10th Sherwood Foresters were in a position of support at the time of the withdrawal, and did not move forward.

Divisional relief came on August 6th when the battalion marched back to Toutencourt. We all expected a period of rest and training for a fortnight or so, for although the line had been quiet - yet even at its very best trench life is a messy undisciplined show, and the men need steady drill and musketry on the range after a few weeks of trenches. Everyone was surprised when the battalion was put at an hour's notice to move, for nothing had been heard of a 'stunt' in the immediate future. However, on the next day - August 8th - the Australians freed Amiens by their great push, and the 17th Division moved down into a position of tactical reserve for the battle. The battalion marched to Daours on the Somme, and feasted their eyes on huge cages full of Boche prisoners. The next day they marched eastwards through Corbie to Vaux-sur-Somme, arriving about midnight, and bivouaced in the fields in the vicinity of the village.

Two blazing hot days were spent here; there was much bathing and lying about in the delicious shade. Very little was heard about the battle which had just taken place on this front; its extent or ultimate object had not been explained; therefore there was a great deal to do and to find out when orders arrived on August 12th to relieve troops of the 11th Australian Brigade the same evening in the line immediately south of the river Somme. This line at the time ran east of Mericourt-sur-Somme, southwards - immediately east of Proyart. The enemy had been driven back to some high ground where he had made a stand. Our forward posts were very shallow affairs, and no attempt was made to wire these as a further advance was expected to be made in the early future. The country behind our front line was cut up with a series of fairly steep valleys running north and south at right angles to the Somme. German huts, most of them sunken into the ground , were in all these valleys; ammunition dumps and horse lines all showed how speedily the Hun had quitted the ground.

Early on the morning of August13th there was some local fighting on the immediate left where the enemy rushed a post held by the 7th Lincolnshire Regt., and thereby gained a certain amount of information; the front of the 10th Sherwood Foresters remained intact.

All remained quiet until very early on the 15th About 12.15 a.m. the enemy started a very heavy gas bombardment on the whole area occupied by the 17th Division; mustard gas predominated. For three hours he kept up a steady stream of shells; he chiefly bombarded the ridges, and as the night was absolutely still the gas floated down into the valleys and clung to the dense undergrowth The area shelled stretched from our support line some 2000 yards westwards, and this all became saturated with the deadly stuff. The sunrise brought with it a ghastly state of affairs; the casualties from the gas poisoning steadily mounted up, and long strings of men with their eyes bandaged, each holding on to the man in front, trailed slowly backwards down to the dressing station. Lieut.-Col. King, D.S.O. [Here the writer pencilled a note in the margin - 'nerves!'] and Adjutant. Capt. G. F. March, M.C. both became casualties, and in all the battalion sustained losses to 18 officers and 519 other ranks; a total which for the moment made it almost cease to exist as a fighting unit; only the garrison of the forward posts escaped the effects of the gas. The large majority of these casualties subsequently recovered, but Lieut. B. G. Barnes and 2nd Lieut. H. E. Merrett died from the effects - both fine plucky officers. R.S.M. Wain also died; his was an almost meteoric career; in March 1916 he was an officer's servant; from that time forward by his sheer ability for making men do what he wanted, and by wanting the right thing, he had risen steadily through non-commissioned rank until he was made R. S. M. in July 1918. Altogether he was one of the finest products of the New Armies, and his loss was felt intensely.

Searching enquiries were made into the reason for the large casualties which the whole division suffered, and much blame attached itself to a great many people; none of them need be mentioned by name.

Major T. W. Daniel took command of the battalion, and Capt. R. O. Nevitt assumed the duties of Adjutant. Reinforcements slowly arrived to fill the gaps, but up to the end of hostilities the battalion never got a chance to absorb the new men and to train them.

On August 16th the battalion was relieved by troops of the 5th Australian Division. The whole of the 17th Division seemed merely to have been used as 'stop gap' troops in between the two Australian offensives; and after it is all over the unfortunate 'stop gap' goes back and starts its own battle - 'No waiting between performances!' The battalion on relief marched to Fouilloy near Corbie, thence on the 17th and 18th they moved back to the V Corps again, to Herissart.

II. Beaumont Hamel and Desart Wood

When the 17th Division rejoined the V Corps, some optimists had rosy visions of the troops being allowed to have a little well-earned rest, and after that - going into the line again for a spell of trench warfare, as dull as the one which we had had opposite Beaumont Hamel; of course nothing of the sort was in store for us. It was very difficult for the average regimental officer to realize even to a small extent that we were entering on the last phase of the whole war. The higher command seemed to proclaim their certainty of success in exactly the same old phrases, and the regimental officer would raise a grim smile at the well-known catch words, but would shake his head unbelievingly.

After 24 hours in Herissart we marched by night to Toutencourt knowing very little of the situation, except that this was another move, and that it did not look as though we should get our rest after all.

On August 21st the 21st and 38th Divisions, holding the V Corps front, attacked the enemy and made some progress east of the Ancre and near Beaumont Hamel. In anticipation of further success the 17th Division moved to a position of readiness. The 10th Sherwood Foresters moved from Toutencourt to Hedauville; this move was made at midday on a blazing hot day. The heat seemed to smite up from the ground like a physical blow, and although the march was only a few miles the troops were more than a little exhausted. Bivouacs were made in the orchards near Hedauville, and touch was obtained with the front line. In the meantime about 350 reinforcements had arrived, and the battalion was able to reorganise into three companies.

Major S. Clarke, M.C., D.C.M. from the 7th Lincolnshire Regiment to take up duties of second in command, arrived on the 19th This officer, with his lengthy experience of the Army, proved invaluable in his position, and the combination of Lieut.-Col. Daniel as C.O., Major Clarke and Captain Nevitt as Adjutant in battalion Headquarters was popular and efficient. Major C. H. Page, D.S.O., was at this time at the Senior Officers'School, Aldershot, and on return was transferred to the 7th Lincolnshire Regiment as second in command.

On the night August 22nd/23rd the 17th Division took over a portion of the line and became the centre division of the V Corps, facing Thiepval. The 50th Brigade held the Divisional front. Very early on the 24th this brigade by means of a magnificent attack captured Thiepval, and by the end of the day held the site of Pozieres.

The 10th Sherwood Foresters as part of the reserve brigade moved to Auchonvillers, and thence in the evening across the Ancre to the vicinity of Thiepval. The roads and especially the makeshift crossings over the Ancre were very much congested with traffic; away from the roads the ground was covered with wire and shell holes, so that moving was very slow work.

At a Battalion Commanders' conference on Thiepval Ridge, Brigadier-General R. M. Dudgeon, D.S.O., M.C. explained that this was for us probably the beginning of the greatest and the final battle of the war. The 51st Brigade were to move eastwards by night and to pass through the 50th Brigade, then to advance to capture Courcelette and Martinpuich, and to push further on to Gueudecourt. The 10th Sherwood Foresters were Brigade reserve for this operation, the other two battalions were abreast in the front line of the Brigade. The 51st Brigade on August 25th succeeded in capturing Courcelette, Martinpuich and Eaucourt l'Abbaye without much opposition; eats of the last village stiff opposition was met. The battalion was not used in the attack, but remained all day in reserve. Several casualties to officers occurred - mainly from the shell fire which was intermittently intense. 2nd Lieut. Smith was killed, and Lieut. Steel and 2nd Lieuts. Catto and Thomas were wounded. Little progress was made on the 26th.

Very early on the morning of the next day the 50th Brigade passed through the 51st Brigade. They made some progress but were held up on the western outskirts of Flers.

On the 28th the battalion moved to the vicinity of Seven Elms between Flers and Martinpuich.

On the night August 28/29th the 51st Brigade relieved the 50 Brigade in the divisional front, and the 10th Sherwood foresters took over a portion of the western outskirts of Flers. Very early in the morning it was found that the enemy had withdrawn opposite our front; patrols were pushed out who found only a few isolated Huns near by; in consequence the whole line advanced.

Flers and Gueudecourt fell into our hands. When our advanced troops endeavoured to cross the high ground between Les Boeufs and Le Transloy, heavy machine gunfire was opened from the north which prevented any further advance. The right flank of the battalion was badly in the air, and no trace of the 38th Division on the right could be found in spite of the fact that they insisted that they were in Les Boeufs. The enemy had taken up a strong position on the western outskirts of Le Transloy; there was little artillery fire in the forward area, but there were large quantities of machine guns which insistently sniped any movement on the part of our men on the forward slope on which our advanced positions lay. A little further progress was made under cover of darkness, but the situation generally remained unchanged until the battalion was relieved by troops of the 52nd Brigade on the night August 30th/31st. The night was pitch black, and all movements in the forward area were very uncertain owing to lack of landmarks and roads, so that it was at a very late hour that the battalion concentrated in the region of Martinpuich. A certain number of trench shelters and old dugouts made the place as comfortable as could be expected.

The battalion remained here till September 2nd, and on that day the 17th Division captured Le Transloy and Rocquigny. We followed up this advance, forming part of the reserve brigade of the division, and reached Rocquigny on the afternoon of the 3rd.

The 50th Brigade had succeeded in capturing Lechelle and had crossed the Canal du Nord. They were definitely held up by the enemy holding a line of defence about a mile east of the canal. The 51st Brigade were given the task of dislodging him from this line. The wire was thick on both sides of the trenches to be attacked, so that the battle was planned to take place from the north in a southerly direction so as to move down the trench line. The 7th Lincolnshire Regiment were selected for this operation, and the

10th Sherwood Foresters were to hold the entire divisional front while this took place. On the night September 4/5th the battalion relieved troops of the 50th Brigade on the divisional front; battalion Headquarters were situuated in Ytres Station, which attracted a most embarrassing amount of attention from the enemy's 21cm. howitzers. The Battalion M.O., Captain John, was seriously wounded for the second time since the advance began.

On September 5th stiff fighting took place in the positions held by the enemy, but eventually he was dislodged and Equancourt fell into our hands.

The battalion did not move until relieved by troops of the 52nd Brigade on the night 6/7th, when they marched back to Rocquigny. In the afternoon of September 7th a further advance took place on the divisional front, and we had to march wearily back again to Vallulart Wood which we had left only some 20 hours before. On September 9th the battalion moved forward and relieved troops of the 50th Brigade in a position of support north of Desart Wood. There they remained two days in bad weather; Desart Wood absorbed almost all the shelling in the neighbourhood, and the battalion was worried very little. Divisional relief by the 38th Division came on the night 11/12th, and the battalion on relief marched back to a Nissen hut camp at Lechelle.

Up to this point in the advance the Sherwood Foresters had been given no responsible task in the offensive owing to the huge gas casualties sustained in August. Reinforcements arrived in September, and a fourth company was formed.

III. The battle of Gauche Wood

The period out of the line was almost entirely filled up in preparation for the next offensive. As soon as the division was settled in its area, conferences in an unending series from Corps Headquarters downwards were held, warning orders and such like flowed from Brigade Headquarters like a river. But in between conferences and 'pow-wows' we sandwiched a good deal of amusement. The Brigade Concert Party - 'The Merry Muffins' - carried on at a furious pace in a large hut which was crowded every night.

Reconnaissances in the forward area were frequent and much care was taken to perfect the workings of the scheme of operations, for this was obviously to be no ordinary attack.

Briefly, the scheme was that the attack should penetrate to a great depth

- almost two miles; two preliminary objectives were to be captured by the other Brigades, while the final objective including the famous Gauche Wood was allotted to the 51st Brigade. The brigade was to attack on a three battalion front, the Sherwood Foresters to be the right battalion. Even if everything worked like clockwork the operation would be difficult one for the battalion, because the forming up line would be on ground which it was impossible to reconnoitre before the attack, and nothing whatsoever could be seen of the ground east of the enemy's front line.

Zero hour was 5.20 a.m. September 18th On the night before, the Sherwood Foresters moved to their assembly positions north of Heudecourt where final preparations were made. The frontage allotted to the division was about a mile; this lay due east of Ravelon Farm between Heudecourt and Gouzeaucourt, and the attack was due to be made eastwards until the Epehy - Gouzeaucourt railway was reached (2nd objective); the 51st Brigade was then to swing north-east, and after capturing Gauche Wood to hold a salient facing Gouzeaucourt to the north and Villers Guislain to the east.

The attack on the right half of the division went well, and the Sherwood Foresters were able to form up immediately west of the railway under cover of a splendid smoke barrage which rose in great billows on the misty air. From there they attacked at the correct time, passing south of Gauche Wood and gaining their objective facing Villers Guislain. The enemy fought for his positions, but nothing could stop the Sherwood Foresters that morning. Every company distinguished itself; 'A' Company under Captain Brandt started as right support company; they lost direction slightly during the advance and found themselves on the left flank of the battalion; here they saw that the 7th Border Regt. on the left were in difficulties, and accordingly they moved to their help and succeeded in capturing 100 prisoners in a large dugout. 'D' Company under Captain Jacques captured 150 prisoners (dismounted Uhlans) and two field guns. 15 machine guns were also captured.

The Border Regiment on the left met with much fierce opposition in Gauche Wood but finally reached their objective. The 7th Lincolnshire Regiment on the extreme left had still fiercer fighting, but were able to finish their task some hours behind the timetable.

All remained unchanged for about four hours while the enemy sorted himself after the heavy blow he had received. About 1.30 p.m. he put down a heavy machine gun barrage behind the foremost line which we had captured and began a series of counter attacks from Gonnelieu. The Border Regiment were driven out of their front trenches and 'B' Company of the

Sherwood Foresters was seriously threatened. Lieut. Steggall in command of the company and 2nd Lieut. Tack, D.C.M., M.M. were both killed while gallantly defending their positions. The enemy began to make some ground, but 2nd Lieut. G. B. Greenwood, who was in close support to 'B' Company, grasped the situation, and on his own initiative led his platoon in an immediate counter-attack. This was completely successful in re-establishing our line and part of the front line of the Border Regiment; 25 of the enemy were killed, and two captured together with six machine guns. 2nd Lieut. Greenwood was wounded, and received a well-earned D.S.O.. Aided by this splendid work the Border Regiment retook the rest of their own front line, and the night passed with the enemy very much on the alert, and inclined to make half-hearted bombing attacks. Lieut.-Col. Daniel was awarded a bar to his D.S.O., and Captain Jacques received a bar to his Military Cross.

On the night September 19/20th the battalion was relieved by troops of the 33rd Division, and then withdrew to Revelon Farm. Two days rest was given, and then we relieved troops of the 50th Brigade who were holding roughly the perimeter of Gauche Wood. The artillery was somewhat quieter although the wood was still no place to loiter in.

Troops of the 21st Division relieved us on the night 25th/26th, and the whole division marched back to good hutted camps round Manancourt.

The battalion rested here till October 5th The usual amount of training, and especially musketry, was done; there was football, and the 'Merry Muffins' became more and more popular. The accommodation for the battalion was a German built camp for a Corps Headquarters. Needless to say it was distinctly good, and the few days rest did a very great deal to pull the men together more as a battalion, and less as a crowd of individuals.

IV. To Neuvilly and the Battle of the Selle River

While the 17th Division was out of the line the V. Corps front advanced many miles. Away to the south the 46th Division crossed the Canal de l'Escaut, and to the north the operations near Masnieres and Rumilly made the salient held by the enemy at Villers Guislain very acute. Finally he evacuated his positions and withdrew to his last organized defence line on the eastern bank of the Canal de l'Escaut. Early in October the 21st Division pushed him out of these defences, and when the 17th Division relieved the 21st Division the front line was immediately west of Walincourt and Selvigny.

The battalion moved on October 5th to rough shelters on their late battlefield near Gouzeaucourt; here they remained two days, going over the places again where the fighting had been hardest, and having a good gloat over the enemy dead which were in many cases still unburied.

At 2 a.m. on October 8th the battalion moved across the Canal de l'Escaut and took up a position of readiness in the trench system south-east of Bantouzelle. A heavy attack was made by the 21st Division in the early hours of the morning, and the 51st Brigade was prepared to follow up the advance. News quickly came that all was well with the attack, and the Brigade moved slowly forward during the day. On the plateau on which we spent most of the day some idea of the huge battle could be grasped. To the north was Cambrai, burning in parts, and across the valley of the Escaut River our line was marked by bursting shells. A host of church steeples was seen to the east, the first we had set eyes on since leaving Mailly Maillet in August. The 21st Division was held up west of Walincourt. The 51st brigade snatched a little rest during the night at Mont Couvez Farm, but early in the morning moved so as to pass through the 21st Division at dawn on the 9th The Sherwood Foresters were in support to the Brigade.

Before the attack started it was found that the enemy had evacuated his positions, and the advance was pressed without artillery until contact was gained with the enemy, first by a few scattered shots from Caullery and then more definitely on the western outskirts of Montigny. Civilians were found in Montigny and Caullery, left behind by the flying Hun. They were of course overjoyed to see British troops and laid themselves out to be as kind and hospitable as their starvation rations would allow.

The battalion was not involved during the day in any of the fighting which was never very fierce, and the opportunities of cementing the Entente were numerous. There were kisses for all, handsome and hideous, married and unmarried, and the time that could be spared to turn round and talk to the people was very merry indeed.

The last objectives, Montigny and Le Trouquoy, fell into our hands before night, and the battalion was billetted in the former village. The next day, October 10th, the 50th Brigade passed through the outpost line and succeeded in reaching the line of the river Selle some eight miles further on. The 51st Brigade became divisional reserve. We rested in Montigny till October 12th, and then moved to Inchy in support of the 52nd Brigade who were attacking across the Selle. In the afternoon the battalion was moved to the high ground west of Neuvilly. After a heavy day's fighting the 52nd Brigade was driven back to its original starting point, and in the evening they were relieved by the 51st Brigade. The 10th Sherwood Foresters were the left battalion of the Brigade. Relief was a very difficult matter indeed as the 52nd Brigade was somewhat disorganised, and the night was pitch black and wet. The front companies pushed forward as near as they could to the positions held by the enemy and dug themselves in. On the left our men were able to cross the Selle, and dug in in a small quarry on the eastern bank; elsewhere we held the western bank of the river.

In the morning the Brigade demanded accurate disposition maps, but in many cases whole platoons had established themselves in full view of the enemy, so they had to lie absolutely 'doggo' for the rest of the day. The enemy sniped vigorously from windows in the houses of Neuvilly. Capt. R. A. Barker, M.C., was mortally wounded, and 2nd Lieut. Whyatt, M.C., was killed by one of these snipers. Both were fine officers; Barker had been in the battalion a long time and had been commanding his company most ably for the whole of the advance. Selwyn Whyatt had proved most popular and efficient as Intelligence Officer.

The battalion held this line till the night of October 15th/16th and the enemy was quiet. It was observed that he was working with great energy on the defences on the east bank of the Selle, so preparations for the next push were hurried on. On relief by troops of the 50th Brigade , the battalion marched back to Montigny where they remained till the 19th Here details were worked out for the dislodgement of the enemy. The 17th Division were to co-operate with many other divisions on the right and left; the 50th Brigade were to penetrate about 1200 yards east of Neuvilly, and the 51st Brigade were to pass through them and penetrate another 1200 yards, capturing Amerval. The 51st Brigade were to attack with all three battalions abreast, the 10th Sherwood Foresters to be the left battalion; they were given a further objective some 800 yards further ahead to conform with the plans of the division on the immediate left. Zero for the start of the attack was 2 a.m. October 20th. After dark on the 19th the battalion moved to their assembly positions between Inchy and Neuvilly; a full moon covered by clouds made the conditions ideal by assembly, but a misty rain made things uncomfortable. The usual crackling din broke out at zero; the whole countryside seemed to be spitting flame. Through it all the battalion moved down the steep slope to the Selle; things were evidently going well for no trouble was coming from Neuvilly. The wooden bridges thrown across by the engineers were all in places, and the battalion was quickly over, and on to their assembly position which was the railway running parallel to the river. From here at 3.50 a.m. we advanced up the hill through the 50th Brigade who had firmly captured their objective. Some opposition from isolated machine gun posts was met with, but the men were out for blood and killed a great number of Boches. The general objective for the Brigade was captured up to time, but the special objective allotted to the battalion was not captured until 4 p.m. and fresh artillery action had been arranged, owing to the 5th Division being held up on the left. All remained comparatively quiet after the final objective had been reached; the enemy was considerably disorganised by the attack, and our men were only too glad to get the chance of a few minutes' sleep, for they had had no rest the night before. The weather kept very lowering and the going became heavy although little rain fell after midday. In the attack 2nd Lieut. Franklin was killed, but casualties were on the whole light; about a hundred of the enemy were captured and a very large number of machine guns. Lieut. P. J. Lynch commanding 'D' Company and Lieut. G. C. Winckly the Signalling Officer both received the Military Cross. October 21st was spent in consolidating the positions gained, and the enemy showed no inclination to attack. It was a very uncomfortable day; everyone felt the reaction after the immense strain of the main attack and they were only too glad to be relieved by troops of the 52nd Brigade on the evening of the 21st.

V. Through the Foret de Mormal to Beaufort

Two days' rest at Inchy were very much appreciated, but events moved at a furious pace in the firing line; the 21st Division relieved the 17th Division and penetrated the enemy positions to a depth of about six miles, capturing Ovillers, Vendegies and Poix du Nord. The 17th Division followed up this attack and took up a position of readiness in the captured area. On October 24th the 10th Sherwood Foresters moved to bivouacs midway between Ovillers and Amerval; a piece of extraordinarily bad staff work

---

Footnote: In this battle the 7th Border Regt. were ordered to capture Amerval and to consolidate on the eastern side of the village; machine guns were very troublesome from the houses, and their C.O. and a Company Commander were killed. The situation was obscure, but the editor of this history (Lieut. W. N. Hoyte, M.C.) who was at the time Intelligence Officer of the 51st Brigade, went forward at once and rallied the company of the Border Regt. which had been temporarily driven out of Amerval. This prompt action saved a critical situation on the right flank of the Brigade. Lieut. Hoyte had just previously been awarded a bar to his M.C. for gallant conduct in Gauche Wood on September 18th.
(T. W. D.)

followed; the battalion marched six miles back to Inchy on the 25th, and retraced their steps to Vendegies on the 26th The marching and counter marching were very trying indeed, the roads were congested with traffic and rain had made movement off the road very difficult. However, we reached Vendegies and rested for three days. The 17th Division held the line, and the 51st Brigade acted as reserve troops. The main difficulty at this time was to continue the maximum amount of training with all the rest the troops required. Drafts of reinforcements had been received during the past month, and there had been little or no opportunity to absorb them properly into the battalion. The task of keeping the battalion in a state of fighting efficiency was enormous; but Lieut.-Col. Daniel, Major Clarke, and all the Company Commanders worked wonders, and the main lack was experience in fighting which cannot be taught on a parade ground.

It was common knowledge that the next big attack would be undertaken by the 17th Division, and at this time details of the operation became known. On the map the Foret de Mormal looked a thick green mass through which any attack would be difficult in the extreme. The broad plan, however, was to push us straight through in an easterly direction until we reached the final objective about half way through the forest. The idea was so impudently daring that even the most optimistic Company Commander was inclined to shake his head, and success seemed almost impossible if the Hun cared to fight at all. Most thorough air reconnaissances were made of the forest and all possible information was published by the Intelligence Branch. To add to the difficulties, the country outside the forest was not open and without hedges like all the rest of France which we had fought over; but it was a mass of orchards, each one separated from its neighbours by a thick high hedge. The difficulties of the attack will be apparent.

A small rest was obtained before Zero Day (November 4th). On October 29th the 21st Division relieved the 17th Division and the battalion marched back once more to Inchy for four days' rest. Final details for the attack were arranged while here. The 51st Brigade were allotted the capture of the 2nd objective; they were to pass through the 52nd Brigade who were to secure the 1st objective on the outskirts of the forest, and were then to advance about a mile due east, and finally to halt on a well marked ride running north and south while the 50th Brigade passed through to capture a further objective. The Sherwood Foresters were chosen as the left battalion of the Brigade.

The front line at that time ran from the eastern outskirts of Englefontaine to Ghissignies; the divisional front lay in between these two villages. The advance was made still more difficult by the fact that although the attack was to be made due east, the line faced north-east. On November 2nd the battalion marched from Inchy to Poix du Nord where they spent a very disturbed night. The enemy artillery (mainly 5.9 howitzers) bombarded the village practically all night so that very little sleep was obtained. The next day a shell exploded just outside the room in which the Commanding Officer was holding his final conference with his officers. 2nd Lieut. Taylor, a very promising subaltern, was hit in the head, and unfortunately died of wounds. R.S.M. Perrons was also wounded. Later in the day forward positions were reconnoitred by Company Commanders, and Capt. A. Kerr was mortally wounded by a shell on the return journey; a most capable officer and good fellow was lost, and further eleventh hour reorganisation was caused.

Altogether our stay in Poix du Nord was a trying one. In the evening of the 3rd we moved forward to our assembly positions about 300 yards behind the front line. Short lengths of deep trench had been dug in a fold in the ground, and the men got what rest they could in these. Zero hour was 5.30 a.m. From about 4.30 a.m. onwards the Hun shelled our front line and the assembly positions, but little damage was done owing to the excellence of the assembly trenches. Zero hour was damp and misty.

The battalion moved forward behind the 52nd Brigade, found that they had little difficulty in capturing their objective, passed through them, and keeping close to the creeping barrage captured their allotted objective to time. It sounds so very easy to do things as they should be done, but the task was not accomplished without difficulty. The enemy artillery shortened their range with most alarming rapidity; in previous attacks the Hun had bombarded the jumping- off line for some hours after our leading troops had left it, and only shortened the range when he had cleared up the situation; but this time the enemy apparently gave up all idea of holding our men in the first mile, and quickly brought back his barrage to the edge of the forest. This caused numerous casualties in Futoy. 2nd Lieut. E. E. Wilson was killed, Lieut. H. E. Hodding, M.C., died of wounds, and Capt. Brandt stopped a huge piece of shell with his leg; 2nd Lieut. H. Street was also wounded.

During the whole of the day the Signalling Officer, Lieut. G. C. Winckley, kept telephone communication with Brigade Headquarters. Considering the weight of the barrage through which his lines ran, the feat was an extraordinarily fine one. For equally good work in the Battle of the Selle he had been awarded the Military Cross; a bar to this was now added. So excellent were the signal arrangements that Divisional H.Q. received a message that the battalion was on its final objective half an hour before anything was heard at all of any other battalion of the 51st or 52nd Brigades.

Sergeant Slack, D.C.M., M.M., who joined the battalion in May with a draft of R.W.F. performed heroic deeds in charge of the linesmen, and for his work on this occasion and during the battle of the Selle he received the D.C.M., and a bar to his Military Medal. Two field guns and a large number of prisoners and machine guns - unfortunately not counted - were captured.

The line of battle moved eastwards like a tidal wave. The 50th Brigade passed through the 51st Brigade, and after stiff fighting gained their objective early the next morning. Soon afterwards the 21st Division passed through the 50th Brigade and continued the advance across the Sambre. The weather at this point broke altogether and rain fell for about three days. Conditions were very uncomfortable indeed as there was practically no covered accommodation. The 17th Division followed up the advance through La Tete Noir, Berlaimont, Aulnoye and Bachant, but the last action of the 10th Sherwood Foresters had been fought. Although the 51st Brigade came into action on November 9th round Beaufort, the battalion formed the supports and took no part in the attack.

An interesting episode occurred in this last battle. At 5 a.m. on the 9th, as the battalion was marched in column of route through Limont - Fontaine which the Huns had evacuated only a few minutes before, many unfortunate inhabitants appeared from the cellars of their houses and saw British troops for the first time since 1914. Greetings were most hearty, and the released civilians hardly knew whether to laugh or cry. After the evening of November 9th the Hun disappeared eastwards, and he could only be found by means of cavalry patrols. The battalion withdrew to Aulnoye on the 9th, and while they were there the Armistice was signed.

Away to the west and in England this event was celebrated in the way that will be passed down to history, but with the fighting troops it was different, for the most part; it was the relaxation of the most tremendous strain which any man could very well bear; the sudden end of all those things - pleasant and unpleasant - which, compounded together, had meant life to us for so many year. There seemed to be so much to be thought out, and so little energy to think with; so most of us solved the problem by going to bed several hours earlier than usual.

Throughout the advance the work of the transport had been magnificent. First under Capt. C. R. Reynard and later under Lieut. C. E. Harvey, this branch of the battalion invariably accomplished its tasks; and in spite of an immense amount of hard work on the roads it always managed to turn out smartly and to look well kept. A few of the original men of the 10th Sherwood Foresters managed to remain as transport drivers during the whole time that the Division was in France. For them no word of praise can be too high. The unknowing often regarded the transport as a 'cinch' and a 'cushy job'; but those of us who saw what the men had to go through every evening near Ypres in 1917 or during the winter of 1916 in the Somme area, know that theirs is a most unenviable task.

A word of praise is also due to the Orderly Room Staff who, although not in the firing line, worked like Trojans to the incessant click of the typewriters, and it was mainly due to their energies that operation orders always reached the companies in plenty of time.

CHAPTER VII
After the Armistice

Few events remain to be chronicled, though much really requires to be said. The 17th Division was not selected to march eastwards to the Rhine, but on November 11th and 12th moved back to Troisvilles, a village close to Inchy. Billets were good but life was peculiar, for there was no 'next push' to look forwards to; the complete silence at night seemed almost uncanny after the continuous rumble of the guns for so many months. Certain branches of the battalion organisation suddenly found themselves with nothing to do, notably the Intelligence officer and Signalling Officer. The Education Scheme was propounded, and 2nd Lieut. E. C. E. Hemsted arrived as Education Officer burning with zeal for other things than killing Huns, and guaranteed to lecture for any length of time on any subject given five minutes' notice. But he unfortunately went sick before all his intentions regarding our education were fulfilled.

On November 25th Capt. G. F. March, M.C., rejoined the battalion, having recovered from the effects of the gas attack in August. He took over the duties of Adjutant from Capt. R. O. Nevitt who assumed command of 'C' Company.

Towards the end of November the authorities announced that the Division was to be billetted in villages near Abbeville, pending demobilization. But they also capped this pleasing news by saying that owing to lack of railway transport we should have to march every step of the way. A period of blank amazement at this news was followed by one in which some quite unprintable opinions were expressed.

In the first days of December came the call for all miners to be sent home to England at once. 191 men left the battalion under this heading, and these included many bandsmen, so that the famous battalion band after a long and tuneful career came to an end. They were very much missed as we marched back to Abbeville.

On December 4th there was a very informal parade of the whole division to cheer His Majesty the King who was visiting the battlefield of the Selle.

The long march started on December 7th, and continued each day till the 13th. We stayed nights at Masnieres in accommodation for Army Headquarters (naturally good), Hermies - a canvas camp, Favreuil - in huts, Albert - a sodden collection of tents, and then billets at Pont Noyelles, Picquigny and Fourdrinoy. The weather was good on the whole, though a grey wet day was spent on the Bapaume - Albert road.

The final billets at Bailleul, Bellifontaine, and Grandsart near Pont Remy, proved to be squalid in the extreme, and after a great deal of argument and bargaining - much better billets were obtained in Epagnette; Pont Remy and Abbeville lay quite close, and officers and men settled down to enjoy to the full their last days in the Army. The Education Scheme was started with much willing support from both officers and men, but it never really flourished as demobilization started almost at once, so that the instructors and instructed were always liable to disappear with practically no notice at all.

Life became very humdrum; there was always someone's farewell dinner either to look forward to or to recover from, and numbers dwindled steadily. Christmas Day was spent cheerily; the men were given a good dinner at midday and this was followed by a concert and performance of the 'Merry Muffins'.

On January 16th, 1919, there was a presentation of colours to the three battalions of the 51st Brigade by the Divisional Commander - Major General P. R. Robertson, C.B., C.M.G.; the ceremony passed off without a hitch. The colours are now deposited in Nottingham Castle.

Demobilization proceeded steadily, and numbers were further thinned by four officers and about 100 men leaving to join Prisoners of War Companies early in April. Successive moves to Cocquerel and Fontaine (close to Pont Remy) were made.

Finally the battalion was reduced to its 'cadre' strength, and on April 23rd they entrained at Longpre for Havre. From here they crossed on the

26th to Southampton, and after a very tedious journey reached Catterick Camp for final demobilization.

The actual chronicling of events ends here, but it is quite impossible to close it without recording in some way the work of many officers and men which has not before been mentioned. This lack of mention has not been because it was not good work, but as it never called for superhuman courage or physical discomfort equal to that of the ordinary man in the ranks, no place seems to have been suitable in which to record it.

Capt. Pearsall, the Quartermaster, was the head of this band of world's workers; he certainly was no ordinary Quartermaster; without his astuteness and faculty for doing the right thing at the right time the battalion would on many occasions have gone hungry, worn ragged uniforms, and gone without the scores of little things which the stores always seemed to have. But nothing that I can say can show how very vital to the battalion organisation was 'Willie' Pearsall.

Luck never dealt out to him any distinguished decoration, but if it is any consolation he can safely rely on the gratitude and the affection of all the officers who were at one time or any in the battalion.

Other members of this band were the Regimental and Company Quartermaster Sergeants, chief among them being 'Jerry' Hickman who succeeded the mighty Soden as R.Q.M.S.

SO CLOSES THE TALE

Author's Apology

Much must be said in small space. First, apologies to all concerned for presuming to write the history at all. The other two officers who were competent for the task as having served for long periods with the battalion definitely refused. Undoubtedly the history had to be written, so at their request and with much help from Lieut.-Col. T. W. Daniel, D.S.O., M.C., I took upon me the task.

I was only actually serving with the 10th Sherwood Foresters from February 1915 to March 1916, but for the remainder of the war I served in an unofficial capacity with the 51st Brigade Headquarters with short periods with the H.Q. 17th Division and 50th Brigade, so that I was during the whole time in fairly close contact with all the goings and comings of the battalion. Particularly I would ask the pardon of all concerned for the use of the word 'we' in connection with the battalion when I was not actually serving with it.

I fear I have proved myself a bad historian, and I have consistently avoided any points of controversy which arose during our existence, and also there are no adverse criticisms. Officers and men, if they are mentioned in the account, are either praised according to their worth or dismissed without comment.

I took up my pencil to write unwillingly, and not until I had progressed some distance did I find how very real was my affection for the old battalion. This affection has more or less tinged the whole account, and made adverse criticism impossible.

W. N. Hoyte